Daddy God

Healing The Orphan Spirit

"A population that does not take care of the elderly and of children and the young has no future, because it abuses both its memory and its promise."

Pope Francis

Dr. Jerry A. Grillo, Jr.

FZM Publishing
Copyright 2016
Daddy God
Healing the Orphan Spirit
Revised & Updated

By **FogZone Ministries**
P.O. Box 3707 Hickory, NC. 28603
www.fogzonedesigns.com

All scriptures, unless indicated, are taken from the King James Version.

Scriptures quotations marked NJKV are taken from the New King James Version.

Scriptures quotations marked NIV are taken from the New International Version.

The Message Bible; THE MESSAGE: The Bible in Contemporary Language © 2002 by Eugene H. Peterson. All rights reserved.

ISBN

978-0-9891997-7-3

Printed in the United States of America

Table of Content

Foreword   5

Acknowledgement   9

Preface   11

My Story   13

God Our Father   19

Overcoming the Orphan Spirit   33

Fearfully and Wonderfully Made   53

Keys to a Successful and Fulfilling Life   67

Slaves No More   73

God is Dedicated   81

God is Affectionate   93

God is Determined   107

You Will Not Be Denied   119

Be a Good Steward   131

You Are Always on His Mind   139

Conclusion   145

Decision Page   149

FOREWORD

Dr. Jerry A. Grillo's book, *"**Daddy God**"* is an important book with a message that is simple, direct and critical for our times. It addresses the most basic issue for the emerging generation, but it is also the crucial message for all ages. It is the message that Jesus came to earth to share with us; He came to reveal the Father.

One of the great shocks I have received in ministry came after I had told those who had gathered for the beginning of our church in Charlotte that we were called to be a family. The shock came when several people came up to me afterward to state how disappointed they were about having to become a family. The very word brought pain to them! These were mostly affluent, upper middle class adults. These people looked and seemed to be in great shape, spiritually, emotionally, and physically. Observing the rest of the people who were gathered, I realized that they were probably some of the most stable, seemingly mature Christians of the whole group.

As I thought about this group who were affluent members of a great city in the strongest nation on earth, I realized that they represented a much larger number of people that are repelled by the very word "family." I knew then that the whole world was in much more trouble than I had realized. I became profoundly thankful for the great ministries that the Lord had raised up to focus on the family. This truly is one of the most important issues of our time. When there were just two brothers on the entire earth one of them basically said, "This place isn't big enough for the both of us!" All human relations are hard—most of them do not work and end up bad, even in the church. The reason they fail is that the most foundational of all relationships - our relationship to the Father - has not been fully restored.

In a sense, the church is our spiritual mother. However, I think as a direct relation to the present state of the average family in America (which is to be without a father), few churches seem to know how to relate to God as a Father. We talk about Him, sing about Him, and bombard Him with our requests; but mostly, we try to avoid Him. One of the enemy's most powerful assaults on humanity is directed at blurring the distinctions between men and women. Through this deception, he has veiled our need for the most important relationship in every life, our relationship with our Father in heaven.

Hebrews 4:15-16 says of Jesus, *"For we do not have a High Priest who cannot sympathize with our weaknesses, but was in all points tempted as we are, yet without sin. Let us therefore come boldly to the throne of grace, that we may obtain mercy and find grace to help in time of need."*

This is an amazing exhortation, but is basic to a victorious Christian life. When we fall short and need the grace and mercy of God, everything in us wants to run from Him just like Adam and Eve did. It is basic to our victory over sin that we learn to run to Him instead of away from Him when we sin. It is also essential for our victory over broken relationships that we learn to run to the very ones that we want to run from.

The Lord hates divorce because it is the perpetuation of sin and defeat. It is the gaping, bleeding wound that all of humanity suffers from. Therefore, one of the highest goals that every husband and wife should have is to keep their vows to remain united until death. This is a basic reflection of our integrity to keep our word, and a reflection that we have walked in union with God. Without God, this is becoming increasingly difficult to do.

One reason why many Christians fail to have a real relationship with their heavenly Father is that they view Him as the angry God of the Old Testament who would smite us all, if it were not for Jesus. There is one thing we must get straight about this—it was the Father who so loved the world, that He gave His only begotten Son to save it! The Father loves us that much! The entire message of the Son of God when He walked the earth was about the Father. His purpose was to restore the relationship between man and the Father. We can only approach Him through Jesus and by the blood that He shed for our atonement. This was done to restore our relationship to the Father. We have not experienced the full purpose of redemption until our relationship to the Father is restored.

Just as the word "family" is a painful, negative word to so many, the very word "father" is equally negative and painful to possibly the majority of people worldwide. Being a father is one of the toughest jobs on earth, and there are very few who are doing it right. No one is doing it perfectly except our Father in heaven! A human being could never have a more wonderful and fulfilling relationship than one with the Father. We were created for this relationship with Him first, and until it is first in our life, no other relationship that we have is going to be at its full potential. I expect this book will help many along the way to achieve this most basic human purpose.

Rick Joyner
Founder Morning Star Ministries

ACKNOWLEDGMENT

I want to acknowledge my own dad and thank God for all the times he has been an inspiration to my family and me. My earthly dad has never had a selfish bone in his body when it comes to giving to his children. He has been the source of who I am!

I want to thank him for the times when I was little for giving me the memories of what someone is like when they have a passion for God.

My father would stay up all night to study God's Word. Through his life's example, he has created in me the desire for the Word of God and His people.

Dad, I love you!

PREFACE

This book is written for the sole purpose of explaining the rights of God's children. We are not in any way trying to promote a disrespectful approach or attitude toward God.

We believe that God is the creator of all things. We believe that God should be approached totally in alliance with the Word of God. When we make the statement "Daddy" God, we are in no way implying that you can run up, jump in God's lap, and pitch a temper tantrum to get what you want. That is not the purpose of this book.

This book deals with the curse of illegitimacy, to set the captives free from the bondage of their past and to explain to the innocent that they are not illegitimate. That was what their parents did, not them. A child born into this world is innocent and no accident. God has a purpose for every human being.

It is my desire that, by the time you finish this book, you will have a clear understanding of who you are and whose you are. You are a child of God. With that birthright comes birth privileges!

It's time for you and me to start claiming our birthrights!

Dr. Jerry Grillo, Jr.

MY STORY

I accepted the call to go into the ministry in 1981. When I started in the ministry, my assignment was youth. I headed off to Lakeland, Florida, where I was going to begin my training as a called Man of God. While I was attending *South Eastern Bible College* (now known as South Eastern University), I was offered a part time position as a youth pastor at Westside Assembly of God. Excited and full of joy, I accepted the position. I was not prepared for what was about to take place in my life. Now, thirty-four years later, I would not trade it for the world. It was these small beginnings where God began to forge me into the man I am today. Many things have happened since those early days, but there seems to be one defining condition that has not changed. This is the attack on our generation of youth that causes them to have an identity deficiency. The crisis has become epidemic. It is not only in our youth; it has grown and that spirit has migrated into our adults and parents.

Identity deficiency

When you have no identity of yourself or your self-image, you begin to follow anything that makes you feel accepted and wanted.

Westside Assembly of God was an experience I will never forget. It was there where God taught me most of what I know today on how to heal the "Orphan Spirit."

The one thing I learned was that I am not normal and my ministry philosophy is not either.

It is as true today as it was back then. People are looking for someone to identify them as being "someone." Truth - **"Everyone is someone to God."**

From adults to children, people need love; they need to know someone cares. They need to feel acceptance. The greatest ministry is not how many you speak to in a crowd but how many you touch in a conversation.

If you want to build any business or ministry then you had better get into the habit of CALLING PEOPLE WEEKLY, HANGING OUT WITH THEM and PLAYING GAMES WITH THEM. Those who you have hung out with on the playground of life, will eventually have no problem sitting with you in church.

Westside Assembly of God was the place where I learned how to touch people with nothing but God's love, especially youth. The years in Lakeland, Florida, proved to be the years of information, growth and heartache. Through it all God showed me what it takes to answer the call, and then stay faithful to that call no matter what.

In 1992, I moved to Dothan, Alabama, and became the youth pastor at North Side Assembly of God. Once again, I accepted a position that had little to offer me in the area of finances, much less any youth ministry. Isn't that really how God works? He leads us to places where we need Him to make it happen. North Side had seven young people. Attendance reached 30 by the end of the first year. By the end of the second year, we were becoming a **powerhouse** for God. Our ministry name was **Soldiers of the Light**. Our motto was *"Love is our weapon; the Holy Ghost is our might."*

We were experiencing rapid growth both spiritually and numerically. Our group of 80 – 90 was taking the city by storm. We were experiencing gang members receiving Christ. Young people living in poverty were finding God, going home, and bringing back their mothers and fathers. My youth were calling me all hours of the night wanting me to pray with them. I had students all over the city wanting to start Bible studies and prayer meetings in their schools. *When* *young people are begging you to come to their schools and pray with them, get ready to have **a God Encounter!***

It all began when I started following the school buses after school to see where the youth lived in my area. I had no idea that when I started visiting those youth that God was going to give me such favor in the local community. Kids were coming to the Lord, and the next week they would bring their brothers or sisters to the youth service. There brothers and sisters would get saved, go home and lead their parent, or parents to the Lord. Those youth were the biggest evangelistic voice in that church. Soldiers of the Light grew that church, the children's church and was taking the community for God.

The quickest way to build a small church is to go and rescue the local youth. When they start coming in they will turn your church and city upside down!

THE BIRTHING OF DADDY GOD:

One Sunday night in church service as the pastor was preaching on how awesome, loving and gracious our Father God is, I gazed out across the congregation and was stunned at the looks on most of the young peoples' faces. These kids were not the normal kids. Most of the time they were into the preaching and shouting and dancing, during

> **Anyone Can Be A Father; It Takes Someone Special To Be A DADDY.**

praise. However, while the pastor was preaching about God as Father, those energized and excited kids were sitting there lifeless, listening with cold and callous stares on their faces. I was shocked and confused. My mind was racing with all kinds of thoughts. All of a sudden, I heard the voice of the Lord say, ***"How can your youth identify with what your pastor is preaching? Most of them have a life without a*** *dad."* I realized that 80 percent of my youth group had either no dads or absentee dads.

That night I found no rest. I kept waking up seeing their hurt eyes. The pain that was screaming through their faces was deafening. I was hurting for them. I had a doctor's appointment scheduled that next morning. While sitting in the waiting room, I noticed a plaque on the wall and walked over to read it. My heart began to break as I read, *"Anyone can be a father, but it takes someone special to be a daddy."* As I was sitting there, I realized what God was trying to say. So many children today are the result of one night of passion and uncontrolled lust. Men are sowing seeds they themselves are unwilling to raise. Fathering children is not hard; just find a woman who can carry your seed.

DADDY GOD!

We live in a time when numerous children each night will go to bed saddened and broken hearted because they want know who and where is there daddy. Why didn't He love me enough to stay with me? Whom do I really belong to? If my own dad did not want me, why would anyone else want me? The orphan heart cries!

Men, listen to me.   When you are sitting on the couch, your children ask you to do something with them and you sacrifice your time for theirs, **you just became their daddy**. When they are on the practice field, or playing a game, and see you in the crowd cheering them on, **you just became their daddy!** When they are lying in the bed and you decide to go in their room and love on them and tell them how much they mean to you, **you just became their daddy!**

Mothers decide what we believe. Dads decide what we remember!

I could not imagine what life would be like not having a daddy. I know that dads aren't always perfect and that sometimes we wonder why they yell or get mad at small things, but I still couldn't imagine life without having an earthly dad.

What kids need more than shoes and clothes is a daddy who will take the time to love them, hold them and identify with them. Fathers could do more for their children by being real and loving than if they bought them the entire world.

What is being echoed in the sounds of today's youth? "Where is my daddy? Who is my daddy? I want my daddy! I miss my daddy!"

We may never restore the physical daddy. You may never know your physical dad. The truth of the matter is, I do not have all the answers about how to restore a physical father.

However, the purpose of this book is not to bring back something in the natural, but to educate you to the supernatural. We all have a **supernatural DADDY**!

- He is a wonderful <u>Daddy</u>!
- He is an awesome <u>Daddy</u>!
- He is a caring <u>Daddy</u>!

He is not afraid to identify us, nor is He ashamed of us! He is DADDY GOD!

CHAPTER ONE

GOD OUR FATHER

In our churches, schools and work place there is a society that is functioning, surviving and existing with no understanding of their self-worth or their real identity. Many people who lack self-worth and identity have a wound that keeps people from recognizing their uniqueness and their distinctiveness. They really do not know what their true personality is. There is such a void in their emotions that they strive to be someone else. They are always attempting to be the person they believe people want them to be and not the person that God has intended for them to be. This is where the problem exists. You can never be fulfilled in life attempting to be what others want you to be; trying to make them accept you for what you do and not for whom you are. Our image is usually discovered by the Father; we tend to want to be who are daddies were.

IDENTITY IS IMPORTANT

Developing a sense of self, or an identity, is an essential part of every individual becoming mature. Identity, or parts of identity, may be classified by any number of things such as religion, race, sexual preference, gender, and/or ethnicity. Some traits are set at birth such as race and sex. Some traits may be modified later in life such as language(s) spoken or religious preferences. Struggling with various parts of identity is natural and normal. Developing an identity, or sense of self, and those traits a person desires to have can take time and may be challenging. Not having a strong sense of self or struggling with identity issues may lead to:

- *Depression*
- *Anxieties*
- *Fits of anger*
- *Hopelessness*
- *Addictions*

- *Health problems*
- *Relationship issues*

When we are void of the power of a father connection in our lives, we begin to question our own existence and values. A strong identity emerges not only from this connection with our father but it is also from a conscious contemplation of our life's purpose. When we have a strong connection to the father, we should develop a strong identity in our adolescence. This creates a strong sense of trust in infancy, autonomy in toddlerhood, the ability to play as a preschooler, getting along with others, and solid work ethic in the elementary years. The issues of childhood may re-emerge later in life as well. Having no father image to compare to may bring problems in your connection to work in your young adult years.

Identity crisis may occur at any time in your life, especially when faced with a challenge to your sense of self. The absence of a father causes you in those tough times to reevaluate your own self-worth and self-image. To be understood, you do not just have to be a child who did not have a father at home, but you could have had a father who did not really connect to you in the way you needed him too. The lack of this connection causes some people to remain all through life in a permanent state of identity confusion.

CURSE OF ILLEGITIMACY

Men and women in the heat of passion cannot control their lust and in the process, they will conceive a child or children. We are experiencing an epidemic in this situation. Many men in our society will sow their seed only to then walk away from these relationships and never look back, leaving these fatherless children without an identity or name.

In the natural, they are labeled "bastards." Webster's dictionary defines "bastard" as **an illegitimate child.**

Illegitimate has a hard meaning to it. It means unlawful, illegal, criminal, wrongful, and illicit. I have strong feelings about a label being placed on an innocent child who had nothing to do with being born. It is wrong to label a child with this term.

What their mother and father did was illegitimate, wrong and illicit. Having a child and not facing the responsibility of their consequences is illegitimate. The child should never be labeled this way!

THE ENEMY IS USING THIS TO CURSE A GENERATION.

In Deuteronomy 23:2 *"One of illegitimate birth shall not enter the assembly of the Lord: even to the tenth generation none of his descendants shall enter the assembly of the Lord." (NKJV)*

I believe one of the major reasons we are having such a hard time connecting this generation into the assembly of the Lord's house is because Satan is using this verse against those who are fatherless. We need to stand up in the power of Jesus' name and verbally break this curse in the minds of this generation.

YOU ARE NO ACCIDENT!

Children born outside of marriages are not a mistake.

The following scripture gives us a reason to believe in every person...

"For I know the plans I have for you, declares the LORD, plans to prosper you and not to harm you, plans to give you hope and a future." Jeremiah 29:11 (NIV)

FIRST STEP TO HEALING

If you are a person who has been in this kind of a situation, your first step to healing is to understand that you are not an accident and that God has a plan for you. God has a strategy for your existence. God is your spiritual Father and has not left you without an identity.

Notice in *Jeremiah 29:11;* God declares that God the Father has a plan for you! Not only does the Father have a plan and a strategy for your life, He also has designed His intention in you. God's intention in you is His anointing for purpose. You are alive because God has put into your DNA a code to live, to win, to outlast and survive. This all happened the very day of your conception. God already decided your whole life. God already put value, importance, and significance into your subsistence!

You may be asking, "What are those plans?" According to the Bible, they are...

1. Plans to prosper you.
2. Plans to make sure you would increase to your full potential in life.
3. Plans to protect you *(not to harm you).*

What a loving and merciful Father He is! God prepared a way for us at the day of our conception!

HOPE IS THE WEAPON THAT DISSOLVES FEAR.

Let's look back at the first chapter of Jeremiah and see what God said about him.

"Before I formed you in the womb I knew you; Before you were born I sanctified you; I (GOD) ordained you a prophet to the nations." Jeremiah 1:5 NKJV

According to this verse, our assignment was decided for us. God ordained us and sanctified us before our earthly fathers could even sow us. God was our Father before He sent our seed to this earth. If our earthly father never saw our greatness, our purpose or our worth our Heavenly Father did. God put a hidden weapon in our hearts. That weapon is hope.

God said in Jeremiah 29:11 His plan was to give you *hope* and a *future*. Without hope, there is absolutely no chance for us to have a future. I believe it is more meaningful to note they are plans to give you hope - not to a future - but *for your future*. Whatever the present situation is in our lives, God has planned for us something better. We have a promise that tomorrow can and will be better than today. I remember hearing that we do not know what tomorrow holds but we know who holds tomorrow. God does.

You have a future that is better than what you are experiencing now! What keeps us moving forward? What keeps us showing up and living? Hope does. Everybody needs hope. Hope is a powerful weapon.

FAITH DOES NOT WORK VOID OF HOPE.

Faith is built upon hope. Man can live thirty days without food. He can even live seven days without water, but he cannot live one second without hope. Hope is defined as expectancy. **Hebrews 11:1** helps us understand what faith is.

"Now faith is the substance of things hoped for, the evidence of things not seen." **Hebrews 11:1 NKJV**

Let's look at another verse that I believe will help us go even further to complete your healing.

"I praise you because I am fearfully and wonderfully made; your works are wonderful, I know that full well. My frame was not hidden from you when I was made in the secret place, when I was woven together in the depths of the earth. Your eyes saw my unformed body; all the days ordained for me were written in your book before one of them came to be." Psalms 139: 14 –16 NIV

You were no mistake! God took time to plan you. God took the time to create you even in the sin of your biological parents! You are fearfully and wonderfully made. This is not an accident on God's part. God saw you while you were just a seed. God knew all about you before you were even thought of by any human being. *Your frame was not hidden from God.* His eyes saw your unformed body and He ordained it with greatness. God knew you before you became a being in your mother's womb.

"Before I formed you in the womb I knew you, before you were born I set you apart; I appointed you as a prophet to the nations." Jeremiah 1:5 NIV

What Parents Do in Moderation, Children Will Do In Excess!

The epidemic number of unwed mothers in this country is staggering. It shows us how Satan has destroyed a whole generation of children. We are watching him destroy the innocence of our youth. What do we do about it? **NOTHING!** What can we do about it? We cannot even get the faithful church people furious enough at the devil to be consistent in their own attendance and walk with God.

As parents, what we do in moderation our children will do in excess. We have become a society who, as the Lord says in His Word, has waxed cold. What use to interest us in the Kingdom of God now agitates us and makes us angry. The mass growing mega churches in the world have become full of people and less full of God's supernatural. We usher people out to pray for them. We are afraid to cast out spirits for fear of offending others. I do not believe the Gospels would have ever been written if Jesus had the same motto as so many trendy churches have.

We wonder why?

- Why is the crime rate soaring for our teenagers?
- Why are our youth dropping out of high school?
- Why are they turning to a life of crime?

I remember speaking at a local prison one Sunday evening. While I was speaking, I noticed a young man sitting hunched over with his face buried in his hands, weeping uncontrollably. I could not get my eyes off him. He was so broken. He was hurting and the pain was leaking from his eyes in the form of tears.

At the conclusion of the service, I went to him and began to minister to him. What he began to tell me floored me. I could not believe it, he was only twenty-three years old. Here he was in prison serving a thirty-year sentence. I was horrified! Here was a young man with his whole life ahead of him, his dreams of getting married, having children, buying a home and growing old with someone and none of it now is possible. His **future** consisted of being locked up for **30 years**. If he serves his entire sentence, he will be **53 years old** when he is released. Right now, my heart is broken again! You want to know what is sad? This story is true all over the prison populations in America.

I am tormented even to this day because I wonder that, maybe someone could have reached this young man. Could we have passed by him on the street thousands of times? Were we so caught up in our daily lives of success and prosperity that we just overlooked his pain, his need to be noticed, loved and cared for? Did we, in our own selfish little world, become so self-focused that we did not even notice he needed someone to tell him about Jesus? How many are we missing and losing daily to the kingdom of darkness because we are so focused on ourselves? We have the power... the anointing... the answer to their problems. But do we notice them?

My greatest fear is what the Father is going to say to us when we get to heaven. Perhaps He will say, *"I loved that new boat; I loved your new car; Wow! What a house you bought."*

Maybe He will say, *"I really was so glad that you missed the gathering of my people when they were coming together to worship me, so you could have fun on that new boat. Did you enjoy the lake; the beach; the mountains?"*

I do not want to stand before the King of all Kings knowing I could have done more and should have done more but just did not want to.

OH HOW THE MIGHTY HAVE FALLEN!

What has happened? I remember a different kind of church in the old days. We used to be a people that would **come early and leave late. Now we come late and leave early!** We used to love being in God's house. We would not miss mid-week service. Now we find every reason and excuse to miss. Then we wonder what has happened to our children? Why are our children rebelling against God? Why don't they want to go to church? Part of the answer is that they see their parents only attend when it is convenient. They question why they should have a passion for something their parents do not.

It is worth repeating that *what we do in moderation, they will do in excess.*

I am living this nightmare right now. As I am revising this book, my wife and I have had to take custody of our first grandchild. She just turned three. I would have never dreamed this would be the life of any grandchild of mine. Last Christmas she did not receive one present from her father, not a phone call, not even a card. How can someone not want to be with her? The other day, she crawled into my daughter's arms, grabbed her face, looked into her eyes, and said, "Mommy, as long as I have you I don't need a daddy."

There are many children waking up every morning without a father. They wonder did he or does he love me? Why did he leave me? Why doesn't he call me and see if I am all right? Was I bad? Am I not good enough? I wish I had a daddy.

LOOKING FOR LOVE IN ALL THE WRONG PLACES.

No wonder our children are engaging themselves in every crime conceivable to man. Our teenagers are crying out for attention. They are looking for some kind of identity! Someone in the church arena needs to speak up and say, "You have been identified and adopted by God!"

Here are some statistics that will drive home the need for us to wake up:

-   In many homes in America, families sit at the dinner table and stare at one another or at the television, or at their cell phones, instead of entering into conversation with one another.[i]

- Most children today get their own selves up for school, make their own breakfast, figure out on their own what to wear and then leave an empty house to go to school. When they return home, they walk into an empty house. They do not enter their homes with the arms of a welcoming mother, not to the smell of dinner in the oven, but to an empty house where the television comforts them and the microwave feeds them.

- The average child between the ages of 6 and 18 will spend between 15,000 to 17,000 hours watching television.[ii]

- By graduation day, the average high school student has seen 18,000 murders in 22,000 hours of television viewing.[iii]

- Twenty-nine percent of 15-year-old girls are sexually active.[iv]

- This number climbs to eighty-nine percent of 18-year-old girls.[v]

- There are 1.5 million abortions each year. [vi]

- The average teen spends 9 hours a day using media.[vii]

- The high school students who dropped out of the class of 2011 will cost the nation's economy an estimated $154 billion in lost income over the course of their lifetimes.[viii]

- A child is abused or neglected every 47 seconds.[ix]

- Infants and toddlers are most likely to be victims of abuse. [x]

- In 2012, 101,719 children in foster care were waiting to be adopted. More than 23,000 youth aged out of foster care at 18 or older without being returned home, adopted or placed with a permanent legal guardian. [xi]

- Over half a million public school students dropped out of grades 9-12 in a school year. This will cost taxpayers in the future billions of dollars a year in added benefits and services and foregone income tax revenue. [xii]

ONE DAY IN AMERICA

- **27 kids die in poverty.**
- **202 kids are arrested for drugs.**
- **340 kids are arrested for drinking.**
- **4,028 children are arrested each day, one every 21 seconds. In addition to this 1,790 children are serving sentences in adult prisons.**
- **1,115 teens get abortions.**
- **101 babies die before age one.**
- **307 kids are arrested for violent crimes.**
- **480 teens get venereal disease.**
- **1,340 teens have babies.**
- **7,940 kids are reported abused and 100,000 are homeless!**[xiii]

In his book "The Bridger Generation," Thom S. Rainer gives some great information about fatherless homes. Mr. Rainer states that...

"The father's role is critical in the (youth) character development. Most criminal offenders come from homes with absentee fathers. In 1970, 86 percent of children under the age of 18 lived with two parents at home. By 1993, the percentage of homes with both parents had dropped to 71 percent. Bridger's today are more likely to live with a never-married mother than were in previous generations. Children of one-parent homes in 1970 included only 7 percent whose mothers had never married. By 1990, 31 percent of single mothers were never married. Thus, bridgers (youth) are increasingly living in fatherless homes, and a growing number have never had a father present."[xiv]

Now is the time for Christians worldwide to begin to seek the face of God and speak up! Tolerance has to end. We must confront these major issues with kindness and love. If there was ever a time in history that we need the church to put down their differences and join in prayer over our cities and nation it is now. We have a generation of people that love Jesus, go to church but deep down inside they really do not know who they are in the Kingdom.

If there has ever been a time to teach people that they are not mistakes, that they do matter, that God has identified them as dearly beloved children, it is now.

CHAPTER TWO

OVERCOMING THE ORPHAN SPIRIT

The very last verse of the Old Testament shares what I believe to be one of the emphasis of the New Testament through Jesus' ministry.

"And he will turn the hearts of the fathers to the children, and the hearts of the children to their fathers, lest I come and strike the earth with a curse." **Malachi 4:6 NKJV**

Luke 1:17 says, *"He will also go before Him in the spirit and power of Elijah, 'to turn the hearts of the fathers to the children,' and the disobedient to the wisdom of the just, to make ready a people prepared for the Lord."*

There is an epidemic happening in the body of Christ. People are not connecting:

- *To the church.*
- *To their spouses.*
- *To their parents.*
- *To the Man of God.*

TEACHERS AND FATHERS

You might think, what is the problem with having more teachers and fewer fathers? Maybe you are saying to yourself that famous scripture right now, *"My people perish for lack of knowledge."* Teachers produce knowledge. This is true; people do perish because they lack knowledge. I am not saying that we do not need teachers or that teachers are evil. I am attempting to address another issue that is in the church and in society. There is emptiness in the hearts of the people for the father spirit.

Teachers attract a different kind of crowd than "spiritual fathers" do. Teachers attract students. Fathers attract children. Teachers create an atmosphere of learning and growing intellectually. Teachers train you for what you are doing, while fathers train you to know who you are. When you know who you are, you will become better equipped to do what you are called to do. Too many people are seeking someone to identify them and prophecy over their future. Few are seeking to connect to a spiritual father.

The Apostle Paul said you have *"thousands of teachers but not many fathers."* (I Corinthians 4:15) People judge you by what you are doing. God judges you by who you are. Most of us have been conditioned to decide who we are by what we are doing. So when you ask someone who he or she is, they won't tell you their name. They will tell you what they do. I am a carpenter, a teacher, a fireman, a police officer, and that is the clue that they are not comfortable with who they are, only in what they are doing.

I cannot tell you how many have made their introduction to me leading with their title before their name. This is especially evident in the church. *"Hi, I'm Elder Jim,"* or, *"Hi, I'm Deacon Joe."* So your name is Elder? Deacon? No, your name is Jim.

The "orphan" wants you to know them by their accomplishments. They have built their value by what they are doing because they really do not want you to know who they are.

When someone is overly focused on their accomplishments instead of their character they tend to be attracted to a voice that stimulates them, encourages them and motivates them. They run from any voice that instructs them, corrects them or desires to train them.

The orphan has a deep need to know their gifting. The orphan is attracted to the prophetic voice because the prophetic voice identifies the gift. People, as a majority, run to a prophet and listen to anyone anywhere from the bathroom to the parking lot as long as they are giving them a **prophetic** word about their skills, giftings and destiny. Do not let a man of God stand up and begin to use words like correction, training, mentorship and qualifications. As long as the leader over them is a teacher, they are comfortable with learning; but if the voice in that leader begins to sound fatherly, disconnection begins to happen. *The orphan is agitated by the apostolic voice - the father's voice - because that voice addresses his character.*

> ## Has Your Gift Taken You Where Your Character Cannot Keep You?

So what does this produce? What is the result in our local churches? We have people in leadership who were promoted by their gifts. *The problem is that their gifts have taken them where their character cannot keep them.* In the end, the Kingdom of God takes the hit. When I say the word "orphan," I am not speaking about not having any parents, or someone who has been abandoned. The **"Orphan Spirit"** refers to a spiritual condition in which some profess outwardly to know God as Father, but experience an internal contradiction to that belief. Spiritual orphans struggle to connect. The word connection carries in it a deep pain and fear in the mind of an orphan. Connection means to bond, to relate and to join. The orphan heart fears this because deep inside their heart they do not see their own value and worth. Because they cannot see their value and worth, they have a hard time believing you really see it either. Somewhere in their past they have picked up the need to be loved. They have a heart of an orphan because they did not receive love – or perceive they did not receive love in their past. Now they have a hard time receiving any love... love from others and especially from a father. It is not that they do not want the love; it is that they have this inner hole in their heart that sees a heavenly Father in relation to their views of an earthly father. They have no issues with running to the cross and accepting the love of Jesus. They know He is our advocator, our intercessor and our covering. They have no problem with the Holy Spirit. He comes as our counselor, comforter and friend. But, bring in the Father and immediately they feel abandoned and rejected. Their mind runs to a big boss in the sky who is judging them, scolding them and ready to cast them to hell because of their sins.

FACTS ABOUT AN ORPHAN SPIRIT:
1. Unable to connect to a spiritual leader.
2. Unable to put down roots or commit to anyone.
3. Change churches frequently. Note the average member only last five years.
4. Someone who is never satisfied or happy.
5. Their faith rises and falls with their feelings.
6. Always looking for something bigger and better.
7. Overly needy for approval and recognition.
8. Someone who is easily offended or hurt.
9. Outburst of uncontrollable anger.
10. Strong feelings of abandonment, even when no one has abandoned them.
11. Easily agitated when given instructions.

WHERE DID THE ORPHAN ORIGINATE?

The first sign of the orphan spirit shows up in the book of Genesis.

"Then the eyes of both of them were opened, and they knew that they were naked; and they sewed fig leaves together and made themselves coverings." Genesis 3:7

What is the first clue that the orphan spirit is being birthed? Self-Awareness! In this **self-awareness** (the orphan spirit), the need for being accepted and the need to be affirmed are born. We see this happening in Genesis with

Adam and Eve. They began to overlook the Father's instruction. They lost perspective and forgot that the Father's view of them was more important than what others saw in them and what they saw about themselves. Adam and Eve lost their identity; they lost their image in the Father and became a 'self-imaged human being. *Self became the center of attention.*

We are so focused on self-image that we forget that we are made in the Father's image and likeness. Adam and Eve did not have to prove who they were, because they should have known whom they were connected to. They lost their God image and traded it for a **"self-image."**

The proof of an unhealthy self-image is when you are always thinking about you. **"How does this affect me?" "What does this mean for me?" "What am I going to get out of this if I do it?"** It's all about Me!

There is danger when we have an overly focused view on prosperity.

Keep reading before you jump on the bandwagon of downing prosperity. I am not downing, nor am I discouraging, people from the law of sowing and reaping. The law of sowing and reaping is in the Bible, and it is a gift given to us by God. However, there is danger in this gift. If all we do in the Kingdom is based only on what we can get from the Kingdom, we have not shifted from the "orphan" to the "Sons of God" (children).

I believe in sowing my seed for a desired result. I am an avid seed sower, but what about doing things in the name of the **cause of Christ**? Where are those who are like Shadrach, Meshach and Abednego? Where are the Daniels, and the Samuels? Where are the Davids and others who did what they did because they had a high love and admiration for God? David got angry when he heard what Goliath was saying about His God. His heart and love for God could not just stand there and listen to Goliath's insults.

"And a champion went out from the camp of the Philistines, named Goliath, from Gath, whose height was six cubits and a span... Then he stood and cried out to the armies of Israel, and said to them, "Why have you come out to line up for battle? Am I not a Philistine, and you the servants of Saul? Choose a man for yourselves, and let him come down to me. If he is able to fight with me and kill me, then we will be your servants. But if I prevail against him and kill him, then you shall be our servants and serve us." And the Philistine said, "I defy the armies of Israel this day; give me a man, that we may fight together." When Saul and all Israel heard these words of the Philistine, they were dismayed and greatly afraid... And all the men of Israel, when they saw the man, fled from him and were dreadfully afraid. So the men of Israel said, "Have you seen this man who has come up? Surely he has come up to defy Israel. And David said, "What shall be done for the man who kills this Philistine and takes away the reproach from Israel? For who is this uncircumcised Philistine, that he should defy the armies of the living God?" ... And David said, "What have I done now? Is there not a cause?" Taken from I Samuel 17 NKJV

David said, "IS THERE NOT A CAUSE?"

David had a high admiration for the name of God. What about us? Shouldn't we have some resemblance of this kind of love and admiration? When the three Hebrew men stood before King Nebuchadnezzar, they did not waver in standing for the things of God. They were quoted saying, *"Even if God doesn't deliver us, we will not bow to your false God...* " They did not stand for God for any other reason but that God was worth standing for.

In the Garden of Eden, the spirit of the **"Orphan"** showed up in the heart of mankind. Now, the orphan spirit has an "all about me" attitude.

Man has become flesh driven. Even today, as Christians, we are supposed to be led by the Spirit but in most cases, it will be the flesh that leads us. What does Paul say? *"Those who are led by the flesh will die, but those who are led by the Spirit are called sons of God."* (Romans 8:13-14)

You are either a "Slave, a Servant or a Son." *(When I use the word "son", I am not leaving out daughters.)*

- Slaves are driven by Condemnation.
- Servants are motivated by Obligation.
- Sons are motivated by Admiration.

FOUR SYMPTOMS OF THE ORPHAN SPIRIT:

God called and designed us to be part of His church family, brothers and sisters in one body together (Galatians 6:10, 1 Corinthians 12). However, having an orphan perspective can affect our relationships in the church. This includes ministry teams and our response to Christian leadership. The orphan cannot overcome their own hurts and wounds to connect to the whole body of Christ. This causes them to stay unhappy and unfulfilled in a family designed culture.

Here are four symptoms of the orphan spirit in church life, along with the Father's corresponding invitation to healing.

1. Competing and Needing to Stand Out.

Spiritual orphans do not feel accepted. They feel the need to prove their worth. This may result in *seeking to hide their own limitations and perceiving the strengths of others as competition. They are secretly taking satisfaction in the weaknesses of others and yet needing the attention of others.*

Our Father's invitation is to a place of unconditional acceptance and rest in our unique, God-given identity. (1 Corinthians 12:18)

Sons and daughters embrace both their strengths and weaknesses - comfortable both with who they are and with whose they are. *They cover each other's weaknesses and joyfully add their combined strengths to the family.* Those who are fully mature in their walk with the Father stand in the gaps of those who are weak. They are not elevated by the failures of others, but they are genuinely hurt when they hear of someone falling.

2. A Desire for Isolation: Individualism

Isolation and independence causes people to withdraw physically or emotionally from others. Deep down the orphan does not feel as though he or she belongs in the family. Suffering a sense of abandonment, the instinct of an orphan is to go it alone. The Kingdom is not an individualist culture. God designed us to be in need of others. We are to use each other to build a wall of love and power through the law of agreement and love. There are so many in the church that have become lone sheep. They do not want to walk with the flock of God and what they fail to understand is that the wolves are watching them. Those who cannot connect to the whole will eventually become wolf's food.

Our Father's invitation is one of welcome embrace, to a place of belonging in His family.

Sons and daughters embrace interdependence—the need of each other. Brothers and sisters celebrate being joined together as family and working as a team. (Ephesians 1:5)

3. A Spirit of Fear and Insecurity

The spiritual orphan is unsure of his or her place in the family. Orphans also feel uncovered and unprotected. Therefore their instinct is to protect themselves and their position. They have this over exaggerated focus on everyone, believing that everyone is against them. Insecurity always births offenses. People who are insecure walk around daily looking and waiting for someone to hurt them. They are so on guard for a fight that they are often sensitive and overly angered when talked to about anything someone else dislikes.

When this happens this produces a spirit that may result in:

- A constant need of reassurance by leaders.
- Lack of confidence in their spiritual gifts, and any ministry position they have been given.
- The need to prove themselves.
- Being protective and territorial about their ministry areas.

Our Father's invitation is to a place of security in His love, care and constant oversight. (Matthew 10:29-31)

Sons and daughters have nothing to fear, already secure in their Father's love and place in the family. They can trust in the Father's faithfulness even when changes or trials occur in church life.

4. Unhealthy Focus on Performance:

The spiritual orphan feels rejected. This causes the belief that he or she must compensate by working hard or performing well in order to be recognized. This may result in:

- A constant drive to perform well. The orphan only believes their value is attached to what they are doing. This is sad because we are not called human doers; we are called "human beings." The orphan heart is consistently driven by the need to be the center of attention because the pain of rejection has not healed. Rejection hurts. I have been rejected so I know the torment you are experiencing if you allow it past your external filter and let it affect your internal self-image. This causes you to never really be in the moment. You will always feel unconnected unless you are being noticed. Your connection is as strong as you are feeling connected. It is impossible for others to always make you feel connected.

- Judging the weaknesses or performance of other team members, family members or leaders. The orphan always knows better. The orphan spirit walks in self-righteousness when it comes to others.

- Having feelings of mistrust towards others - feeling that they are going to be 'punished' at any time.

Our "Daddy" God's invitation is to experience the fullness of His undeserved grace and favor (Ephesians 1:6). Sons and daughters generously extend grace to others' failures to measure up to actual or perceived standards. This is because they know the fullness of the Father's grace towards them and have no problem extending that grace and love to others. Sons and daughters respond well to measurements or reviews in work or ministry, knowing that they exist to call forth the best from the team. [xv]

11 SIGNS OF AN ORPHAN SPIRIT

1. The orphan spirit operates out of insecurity and jealousy. The fully mature "son-ship" functions out of **love** and **acceptance**. Those with an orphan spirit are constantly battling jealousy and insecurity. Security originates in a secure relationship with our parents. Those with an orphan spirit are so insecure that they even have a hard time hearing a biological or spiritual father praise their siblings or co-laborers. When a parent is speaking about the other children, the orphan spirit feels cut, hurt and has no joy in the conversation. This is not to say that they do not love their siblings, but it is how they hear the parent speak praise about them that hurts. The reason is that they are not comfortable being who they are. The insecure feeling creates jealousy and pain. Instead of arguing with that child at that moment, the parent needs to discern and address the rejected heart and love it to become a healed heart.

However, those with the spirit of "son-ship" are so secure *in the Father's love* and favor that they are content to serve in any capacity needed, whether or not they are in charge or celebrated in the process.

2. The orphan spirit is jealous of the success of his brothers or sisters. The mature son is committed to the success of his brothers. Those with an orphan spirit are happy when their brother or sister fails because it makes them feel good about themselves. On the other hand, those with the spirit of "son-ship" joyfully commit themselves to serve, celebrate and help their brothers succeed. They do not work for human accolades but out of a deep sense of the love and affirmation of Father God.

3. **The orphan spirit serves God to earn the Father's love.** The mature son serves God out of a sense of divine acceptance and favor.

Along these lines, those with an orphan spirit are constantly striving and trying to earn the Father's love through **accomplishment** in ministry or career. Those with a spirit of "son-ship" already know they are accepted in Christ and serve others out of the abundance of this acceptance. It is not by works but by faith that we are all saved

4. **The orphan spirit tries to medicate its deep internal alienation through physical stimulation.** The mature son walks in the joy and presence of the Lord for comfort.

Those with an orphan spirit are constantly trying to push down their sense of alienation, loneliness and lack of self-worth through constant work, going from one relationship to the next and moving from one physical gratification to another. Nevertheless, in the end it is never enough because the orphan cannot be satisfied. The orphan heart has mood swings of joy to anger all in one moment. The orphan heart lives in a life of *narcissism and self-indulgence.* However, the more they indulge, the more addicted they become and the larger the hole in their heart becomes. Only the love of the Father can fill the deep emotional needs they have. Every day the orphan always has to fight a sense of sadness and depression. If they go on a vacation, they cannot even enjoy themselves because they are always anticipating the feeling of when it is going to end. Nothing is ever what it is supposed to be. The orphan cannot adapt to disappointments.

Those walking as God's children, "son-ship," bask in the presence and love of Daddy God and practice the joy of the Lord continually as their source of strength. They understand that grounding their security and self-life in anything other than God is like trying to build a house on sinking sand. They have a great GOD SELF- IMAGE!

5. **The orphan spirit is driven by the need for success.** The Spirit leads the mature son into his calling and mission.

Many attempt to accomplish great things to satisfy the deep yearning in their hearts for their father's approval. This results in them being driven to succeed instead of being led by the Spirit.

Even many leaders get their churches into huge debt to build huge buildings, driving the people with them because they are blinded by their own innate feelings of inadequacy. They think they can feel good about themselves with great accomplishments. What they are crying for is Daddy God. Sometimes these children have an over emphasized love for their mother, but deep down resent their father. They may show acts of honor or at times seem to be very in love with their father but these are external shows of a false admiration. Deep down in their heart of hearts they are crying for their poppa.

Only those with a strong sense of Kingdom connection, "son-ship," will allow the Lord to direct them and bring opportunities to them without trying to drum up their own success.

6. **The orphan spirit uses people as objects to fulfill goals.** Mature sons serve people to bless the Kingdom.

Those with an orphan spirit tend to use people as objects to accomplish their goals. Whenever we objectify people, we manipulate them with words, threats and anything necessary to have our way and control them.

Never love things more than people. When you love things more than people, you use people to get things. The orphan cannot stop attempting to fulfill their lives with success long enough to enjoy the life around them. The orphan uses phrases like, *"Are you really supposed to be happy? Isn't happiness attached to what you're doing?"* These are all attempts to explain away why they are not living life. They are only existing in life and hurting because they have no joy. The orphan lives too much in their future so they do not have to face their real life in their present. They will manipulate anyone to do anything they need them to do to keep them happy and fulfilled in the moment.

> **Don't Love Things More Than People.**

Mature people who walk in "son-ship" do not use people. They serve and release people to fulfill their destiny in Christ.

7. *The orphan spirit repels children.* The spirit of "son-ship" attracts spiritual children.

Leaders and parents with an orphan spirit are constantly in turmoil, fighting and striving for their own way. This gives their spiritual children the sense that their leader is in competition with them instead of loving them.

This results in repelling spiritual and biological children, which can forfeit influence over the next generation. The orphan spirit puts an emphasis on partnership more than "son-ship." They are looking for those who will support what they are striving to accomplish, but they do not want to support others in relationships. Orphans can only have one or two close friends at a time.

Those who walk in "son-ship" walk in the Father's anointing and draw children toward them because their children hear the voice of a shepherd who cares for them.

8. *The orphan spirit has anger and fits of rage.* The spirit of "son-ship" rests in the Father's ability to control and guide the future.

Those with an orphan spirit have issues with uncontrollable anger, fits of rage and other forms of manipulation. They feel they must control others and their circumstances in order to fulfill their goals. This is because they lack the trust necessary in their heavenly Father to guide and control their future.

Those walking in "son-ship" walk in the Father's rest and have ceased from their own works so the Father can have His way in their lives.

9. *The orphan spirit is always in competition with others.* The spirit of "son-ship" is always blessing others.

Those with an orphan spirit are always trying to outdo others in their church, family, business or denomination because they receive their identity through being better than everyone else is. Their value is only as high as their last accomplishment. They are overly focused on what they have, drive, live in, wear and do. The sad thing is it is never enough. They will move from one materialistic adventure to another, always avoiding the real issue. This is why they do not feel fulfilled.

Those who walk in "son-ship" are constantly seeing how they can bless others since they already have the affirmation of God in their souls. They want to freely share His love with others.

10. *The orphan spirit lacks self-esteem.* The spirit of "son-ship" walks in the love and acceptance of Father God.

Those with an orphan spirit have a hard time loving and accepting themselves. Those walking in the Fathers identity, "son-ship," are filled with a sense of divine love and acceptance that enables them to walk confidently in the joy of the Lord. This is in spite of the fact that all humans are sinners and fall short of the glory of God.

11. *The orphan spirit receives its primary identity through material possessions, physical appearance and activities.* The spirit of "son-ship" is grounded in "son-ship" and the Father's affirmation.

Those with an orphan spirit never have enough career success, material possessions, pleasures or illicit relationships to satisfy the hole in their heart related to their identity.

Consequently, they are constantly striving to gain satisfaction with various things or people in their lives. In many cases, even their form of dress could manifest in an inordinate amount of tattoos, skin piercings and hairdos. This can be their unique way of standing out in a cry for attention due to a lack of self-esteem and fatherly affirmation.[xvi]

God wants to heal the orphan heart. He has made provision for it through the cross.

'The Spirit you received does not make you slaves, so that you live in fear again; rather, the Spirit you received brought about your adoption to sonship. And by him we cry, "Abba, Father." Romans 8:15 NIV

IF YOU KNOW SOMEONE WHO HAS AN ORPHAN SPIRIT, PRAY THIS PRAYER:

I plead the Blood of Jesus upon (***insert name***) and I bind every spirit of an orphan from their lives. I loose and release the Holy Spirit to hover over them to bring healing and deliverance. Lord, you are their Father and I pray that they will receive the spirit of adoption, (Romans 8:15) and that they will call You "Abba." Lord, I pray that healing will come to every area of their hearts. Where their heart has become stony, I pray that you would make it a heart of flesh (Ezekiel 11:19). Lord, I ask that you will bring committed spiritual fathers into their lives to cover them in prayer, to give them direction and to love them. God, please help this spiritual father to have the mind and heart of Christ! In the name of Jesus, Amen!

IF YOU HAVE THE ORPHAN SPIRIT, PRAY THIS PRAYER:

Jesus, please forgive me for embracing the attitudes, actions and heart of an orphan. Your heart and desire for me is that I am a healthy part of a spiritual family. I break all soul ties I have formed with an orphan spirit in Jesus' name. I bind my body, heart and spirit to God's will and purpose for me, in Jesus' name. Lord, I ask that you would heal my mind and my heart from the spirits of abandonment, rejection and fatherlessness. God, please help me to have the heart of a son, and please help me to turn my heart toward my spiritual father. Lord, please help me to pray for and support the spiritual fathers you have placed in my life. Please help me to model the attitude and heart that Jesus had towards You as He walked this earth. Lord, please reveal to me all areas in my life that have been wounded. Please heal those areas and make me whole. Lord, I ask that you would help me to forgive everyone who I looked to as a spiritual father or leader who wounded me or failed me. Lord, please help me to commit to a church and spiritual father. In Jesus' name I pray, Amen.[xvii]

CHAPTER THREE

FEARFULLY AND WONDERFULLY MADE

"I will praise You, for I am fearfully and wonderfully made; Marvelous are Your works, And that my soul knows very well." Psalms 139:14 NKJV

Deep in the heart of children you can hear them crying out!

"Who is my daddy?"
"Where is my father?"
"Why didn't my father love me?"

One of the reasons I believe that the body of Christ is so anemic, feeble and colorless is because they do not know who they are in the Kingdom of God. They understand going to church, but not walking and living in a Kingdom culture. Questions haunt them. Questions like, *"Why am I here? Why does God want to save me?"* These questions have to be answered before we can take our rightful place in the family of God.

TRENDS ARE MORE IMPORTANT THAN CHANGE

There seems to be a huge difference between the early church and the modern day church. The early church moved in powerful signs and wonders. They were a people full of expectation for the miraculous. There focus was the gospel more than the blessings. Today, the focus is the blessings before the gospel. We have become a generation looking for hype and glitter. The truth is that life is neither! Life is a process of change. Life is time, process, endurance and overcoming obstacles. You must be willing to go through what it takes to change, in the good times and bad, to live life to the fullest.

When people win, they party; and when they lose, they ponder. We learn more in loss than we do walking in victory.

The modern church has become an expert at making people feel comfortable. The majority have become professionals in the "instant" and "I want it now" syndrome to the point that we cannot wait for anything. However, most things in life worth having don't come instantly. In 1970, Stanford University did a study. They asked a group of elementary kids a question and then followed them throughout their lives. The question was, *"Do you want one marshmallow now or two marshmallows later."* The ones that decided to take the two later became more successful than the children that took the one marshmallow now. The difference was the ability to wait. Life is not about instant; it is about process.

God does not fit in the instant as much as we would like Him to. Do not misunderstand me; I am not speaking against those powerful moments when God decides to do something "suddenly." I believe in the "**suddenly**" of God's Word. I preach and expect God to do supernatural things. When God does, they always appear to be SUDDENLY! Those are called miracles. However, there are things that just do not and will not come suddenly.

We call that **"LIFE!"** There are some things in life you cannot just pray away, confess away, praise away or even shout away. Most prayer has been reduced to begging God to do what we are unwilling to do for ourselves. You are going to have to learn to be patient when it comes to change. You will just have to wait and out last your moments!

GOOD NEWS

Here is the good news. Your waiting will not be in vain. It shall come to pass! Just hang on to what God has promised you, and it will come to pass. *Isaiah 40:1* says that your warfare has been completed and you are going to get double for your trouble (paraphrased).

"Comfort, comfort my people, says your God. Speak tenderly to Jerusalem, and proclaim to her that her hard service has been completed, that her sin has been paid for,

that she has received from the LORD's hand double for all her sins." Isaiah 40:1-2 NIV

Whatever you have been suffering through, whatever you have been hurting over, God is about to give you double for your trouble!

For us to outlast our storms and seasons of change there are certain things we must be persistent in. We are going to need to know who our supernatural Daddy is, what is He all about and be confident that He loves me and cares for us. We are going to have to know that the plan of God for our lives is far more important than the miracles He performs.

LIVE FOR PROCESS NOT MIRACLES

Miracles are scheduled to happen in moments. Do not get it twisted. "Miracle Moments" are awesome. I love it when God decides to show up in the process and schedule a miracle in a moment. Life is not a moment; life consists of many moments. For you and me to process to our greater calling, we are going to have to move past moments and start understanding the plan. The plan is what sets the progression for our future to manifest in our now. I believe the plan of the Father for us is the miracle. None of us are accidents. All of us are somebody to God. So if you know the plan, you will discover that in the plan is our miracle. Knowing the plan gives direction; it is easier to set the course of action. What God did to the devil was more than just dying for your sins. He set up a plan for our future, not only in heaven but also on the earth.

"For I know the thoughts that I think toward you, says the Lord, thoughts of peace and not of evil, to give you a future and a hope." Jeremiah 29:11 NKJV

Facts about knowing the plan:

1. The plan creates focus.
2. Knowing the plan keeps the main thing, the main thing.
3. The plan decides action.
4. Knowing the plan makes crisis bearable.
5. The plan decides momentum.
6. The plan crushes discouragement.

NO DISRESPECT INTENDED

Using the term "Daddy" or "Poppa" for God is in no way dishonoring or disrespecting God's divine and supreme power and majesty. God Himself used the term "Father" to describe who He is in the New Testament. Jesus said in His own words that God is our Father. The word "father" is used many times in the Bible. The word "fatherless" is used forty three times. God was referred to as "our Father" thirteen times in the Old Testament. Jesus' frequent use of this title brought a complete new understanding of our relationship with God. Jesus referred to God as His Father over **150 times**, and He spoke of God as being **our Father 30 times**. This infuriated the religious Jews of Jesus' day who considered it blasphemy to call God their father, because they perceived that to mean they were equal with God (John. 5:17-18). It was God that told us to call Him the God of Abraham, Isaac and Jacob. It appears that God is a God of linage and family.

It is not my goal to bring disrespect to the office of the Supreme Being but to adequately open up the honorable office of God as our loving Father, **"Daddy God."** No matter how much God is our Father, He is also a God of order. God has made clear references in His Word on how we must approach Him. What I want to do is to uncover the plan of God as our spiritual parent.

"Make a joyful noise unto the LORD, all ye lands. Serve the LORD with gladness: come before his presence with singing. Know ye that the LORD he is God: it is he that hath made us, and not we ourselves; we are his people, and the sheep of his pasture. Enter into his gates with thanksgiving, and into his courts with praise: be thankful unto him, and bless his name. Psalms 100:1-4 KJV

I was fortunate to run into Pastor Bob Weiner, who is a present day Apostle. He challenged me...and after spending two hours with him, my eyes were open to a deeper walk with God. Pastor Bob began to share with me what I am about to share here with you.

CURSE OF ILLEGITIMACY

In the Old Testament, when someone was born illegitimate, they were forbidden to enter into the assembly for ten generations. I believe one of the most overlooked problems in our churches today is the problem of **illegitimacy**. This is not meant to confuse you with the beginning of this book where I addressed the word illegitimacy. I still believe that the definition of the word illegitimacy should not be given to those who are born innocent. However, in this section I do want to deal with the curse **of illegitimacy**.

We have people sitting in our churches who have never had a daddy or who have never known their daddy. They sit in our services and wonder why they cannot get involved or seem to not fit in to the main stream of the assembly. **The curse!** It is trying to hang on to them; a ten-generation curse!

THE EFFECTS OF A FATHERLESS CHILD

- 63% of youth suicides are from fatherless homes. (US Dept. of Health/Census) This is 5 times the average.
- 90% of all homeless and runaway children are from fatherless homes. This is 32 times the average.
- 85% of all children who show behavior disorders come from fatherless homes. This is 20 times the average. (Center for Disease Control)
- 80% of rapists with anger problems come from fatherless homes. This is14 times the average. (Justice & Behavior, Vol 14, p. 403-26)
- 71% of all high school dropouts come from fatherless homes. This is 9 times the average. (National Principals Association Report)

Father Factor in Education

- Fatherless children are twice as likely to drop out of school.
- Children with Fathers who are involved are 40% less likely to repeat a grade in school.
- Children with Fathers who are involved are 70% less likely to drop out of school.
- Children with Fathers who are involved are more likely to get A's in school.
- Children with Fathers who are involved are more likely to enjoy school and engage in extracurricular activities.
- 75% of all adolescent patients in chemical abuse centers come from fatherless homes. This is 10 times the average.
- Children who live absent from their biological fathers are at least two to three times more likely to be poor, to use drugs, to experience educational- health-emotional-and behavioral problems, to be victims of child abuse, and to engage in criminal behavior than their peers who live with their married, biological (or adoptive) parents.[xviii]

You see the orphan spirit is alive and strong!

My mind was full and my heart was heavy when I returned home from that conference. I could see how Satan is using that old curse to hinder this Christ delivered generation. He is doing it through the Orphan Spirit. That Sunday when I returned to my church, I was led to have all the people who were born, or had children, illegitimately to come to the altar to take spiritual authority over this curse and rebuke the enemy at its source.

I cannot describe in writing what happened that Sunday morning. Almost 75 people came running to the altar. I was amazed at how many came. Then I was reminded about the day I was in the pulpit at North Side Assembly of God and God spoke to me about this very same subject. Most of my youth were from broken homes and most of the people at North Side had the exact same response.

I can tell you this. That Sunday was a momentous day at the Favor Center Church. The Spirit of God was so strong that people did not get up from the altar for hours. In most churches, people are eager to leave as soon as they know service is about to end. **Not this day!** Almost 95 percent of the congregation stayed on their faces crying and forgiving their earthly father wounds. The inner healing that God was doing was enormous. People were experiencing a daddy wound being healed for the first time; asking God to heal them from the deep inner prisons where they locked up all of those pains. God's liquid love flowed through them. I can tell a difference in those people to this day. They have been reborn and renewed. We operated in the supernatural; we took authority over the curse of illegitimacy. When the natural wound is healed, it opens the heart to receive the Heavenly father, "Daddy God!"

IDENTITY CRISIS IS REAL

The identity crisis we face in our churches today is real. I know it is mainly operating under the curse of illegitimacy. We are focused on salvation and making sure someone comes to an altar to confess their sins and receive Jesus, but do we ever even think about introducing them to a spiritual Father. We have them fill out confession cards so that we can boast about how many turned and walked away from sin; but have we considered how well are we raising those young babes in Christ to grow into their adoptions as sons and daughters? I think not!

Jesus brings us to the power. God is our Father, and He is our identity. Many are introduced to the Son but never meet our Father. You do not know who you are until you meet the Father. Spiritual babes who are not fathered properly will grow up and have no identity. They sit in our congregations all over America crying out *Where is my daddy? Who was the one who took the time to birth me, but won't take the time to identify with me?"* This is tragic! This is awful!

We need to do something about it today! We need to take the responsibility to train, love and disciple those we birth into the kingdom as much as into this world.

"BIOLOGICAL DADS NEEDED!" APPLY IN PERSON."

In 1995, 25 million children lived in homes without their biological fathers. The popular opinion was that this would affect boys more than girls. **This is not true![xix]**

"A study of girls ages 12 through 17 found that adolescent girls in fatherless homes were almost twice as likely to use drugs, alcohol, or tobacco than girls living with both biological parents."

"Research has found that girls living with their biological fathers experience puberty later than other girls while the presence of a step-father or a live-in boyfriend in the home actually did speed up puberty. This placed girls at a higher risk for early sexual activity and teen pregnancies."[xx]

Again, this shows us the need to follow the Word of God whole-heartedly, not allowing Satan to dilute the message of the Bible. We must live according to God's laws and precepts daily.

When we start speaking about an enemy, such as Satan and bad things, a spirit of fear creeps in our hearts. This is normal. The proof of faith is when you sense fear. Fear always shows up when faith shows up. When we decide to walk in faith, the fear we are facing has to leave. However, when fear creeps in, the first thing we tend to do is to start questioning our actions. We start feeling a sense of worry, and we wonder where God is. I have been here many times. The identity wound is a powerful and crippling wound. I can testify this first hand. I carried some deep, dark hurts for many years; walking in a dark hallway wondering who I was. Did I measure up? Why had God chosen me?

Let me encourage you to remember the words of Jesus.

"And the seventy returned again with joy, saying, Lord, even the devils are subject unto us through thy name. And he said unto them, I beheld Satan as lightning fall from heaven. Behold, I give unto you power to tread on serpents and scorpions, and over all the power of the enemy: and nothing shall by any means hurt you." **Luke 10:17-20 KJV**

Satan does not have the power to destroy you. He cannot lay one skinny finger on you. The enemy's power over us is not in that he has the power to touch us, but in that he has the power to distract us.

DISTRACTION: SATAN'S GREATEST WEAPON

Distraction can destroy you. *"Most people fail because of broken focus."* Broken focus can break your ability to see the blessing for staring too long at the problem. **Distraction is deadly.** How many times have you almost had a car wreck looking down at your phone to see who is calling you or texting you? That one moment of distraction almost derailed you. In many cases, it has. Looking too long in the rearview mirror is dangerous. We are to glance at where we have been, not study and mediate on it. How many of us

> **Stop Telling God How Big Your Problems Are. Start Telling Your Problems How Big Your God Is!**

have spent hours, wasted hours, crying and regretting our past? All of these events are the power of the enemy's distraction. *What you keep looking at you will eventually believe.* When we take our eyes off the Word of God and focus on the problems around us, we will begin to believe the things we see rather than what the Word of God says. Everybody has to face his or her mountains. God does not want you to complain about it, compromise in it or conform to it! God allows mountains to show up so that you can **COMMAND IT!** Why don't you quit telling God how big your problems are and start telling your problems how BIG your God is!

GOD IS AWESOME

To fix this generation of hurting, dying and fatherless children we are first going to have to make sure we are completely fixed our-selves. It is impossible to help someone if you have not first found help for yourself. If you keep leaking issues, how can you help someone quit leaking their issues? You cannot!

Wounded people leak issues!

God may not have birthed us, but God sure did adopt us. Our identity is found in our heavenly "Dad." We are made in His image according to His likeness!

CHAPTER FOUR

THREE KEYS
TO A SUCCESSFUL
AND FULFILLED LIFE

3 Keys To A Successful and Joyful Life:

1. *Stop Competing and Comparing.*

The greatest pain you will experience in life will be living a life in competition to everyone you know. You will never truly discern your value until you stop competing with others. Life is not a competition; life is an adventure to be lived. When you stop focusing on what others are doing and what others have, you will start enjoying not only where you are but where others are also. There is a liberating factor in life when you can rejoice with others over their success and not feel threatened by them. What makes us feel threatened? We are always evaluating where we are to where others are. Seeing more of what others have keeps us from seeing what we have. God has blessed us and we miss that blessing when we resent others who are being blessed.

2. *Start Discovering!*

Open your eyes and discover the goodness, the greatness and the joy God has hidden in your present season. When you stop competing and comparing, you will begin to discover your own gifts and assignment. Become a pioneer and life traveler. Decide to move in life in places no one has been.

> **Blessed Before You Were Conceived!**

Pioneers make their own paths. Discover that God has already set you up for your destiny. I have learned that you do not decide your destiny; you discover it. God hid it in you before you got to planet earth. Hidden in your mind is a purpose and calling. Remember, Jeremiah 1:5 says, *"Before I formed you in the womb I knew you; before you were born I sanctified you; I ordained you a prophet to the nations."*

Before God formed us, He knew us. God knew us before He designed us, fashioned us and made us. To "know us" means that God identified us, distinguished us and (I love this)...God understood, recognized and appreciated us. Do you see the healing in this? Such an awesome value has been placed in us before we even became us. Why are we attempting to please anyone but our Heavenly Father? We were somebody in His eyes before we were substance in someone else's eyes.

God sanctified us! The word **sanctified** means that He consecrated us. We were already set apart before we were formed by conception, before we were given a body - while we were still in God's thoughts. **Sanctified** means that God laid His hands of blessings on us before we were formed. We came into this earth BLESSED!

We were not just blessed, but we were also **ordained.** Ordained is a powerful word. Ordained means predestined. The word "fate" comes to mind. We are bound to a future. No one reading this book is a mistake. You were in God's intentions before time was even spoken. Your value and worth is greater than anyone has ever told you. No more trying to compete. No more feeling inadequate or useless. No more attempting to be someone you are not. No more orphans!

3. *Start Sowing:*

You are a walking warehouse of seed. Seed is bigger than you have been taught. The church has not done a great job teaching on the seed. When we teach the seed we tend to become one dimensional in its teaching. We only focus on sowing for a financial or material harvest. Yes, God has set us up to be the originator of our own financial harvest. The Bible says that each seed must produce after its own kind. So if you sow or give money and call it your seed, it can only produce after its own kind. Money is what you should reproduce in harvest form. However, there is more to the seed message than materialism. Anything you do that is from your hand or actions can be interpreted as seed. Sowing and reaping can be a positive experience or a negative one. Galatians 6:9 gives us the true value of sowing.

*"Let him who is taught the word share in all good things with him who teaches. Do not be deceived (**misled, tricked**) God is not mocked; for whatever a man sows, that he will also reap. For he who sows to his flesh will of the flesh reap corruption, but he who sows to the Spirit will of the Spirit reap everlasting life. And let us not grow weary while doing good, for in due season we shall reap if we do not lose heart. Therefore, as we have opportunity, let us do good to all, especially to those who are of the household of faith. "*
Galatians 6:6-10 NKJV

The Seed is Bigger than MONEY.

Everything we sow we will reap. If we sow time to eat healthy and exercise, we must expect health and physical strength. If we sow time into our marriages and our children, we must expect a harvest of a good family and great children. If we sow kindness, we must expect that in return. Each seed must not attempt to produce what it is not. This is an abomination on the earth. Dogs are not trying to birth cats. I hope you are mature enough to walk in this. We are not throwing money out. Money is a seed that will produce money so expect it. However, we must be more than just money focused.

Sow every kind of seed you can so you can reap all kinds of different harvests. Remember, bad seed produces the same as good seed. Limit sowing bad seeds. We reap what we sow! Here is where I like to say, "Wrong decisions decide unintended consequences." Wrong seeds will produce wrong harvests as much as right seeds will produce right harvests. The decision is yours. If you do not like the harvest that you are reaping today, then change the seeds you have been sowing.

CHAPTER FIVE

SLAVES NO MORE!

EMPOWERED TO POSSESS MY HERITAGE

"After this manner therefore pray ye: "Our Father which art in heaven, hallowed be thy name...." Matthew 6:9

"The Spirit you received does not make you slaves, so that you live in fear again; rather, the Spirit you received brought about your adoption to sonship. And by him we cry, "Abba, Father." The Spirit himself testifies with our spirit that we are God's children. Now if we are children, then we are heirs-heirs of God and co-heirs with Christ, if indeed we share in his sufferings in order that we may also share in his glory." Romans 8:15-17 NIV

"He will call out to me, 'You are my Father, my God, the Rock my Savior.'" Psalms 89:26 NIV

"...because the LORD disciplines those he loves, as a father the son he delights in." Proverbs 3:12 NIV

KEY WORDS

There are four key words in Romans 8:15. Those words are Received, Adoption, Abba and Father. Taking a closer look at these four key words will help us gain a deeper and more powerful understanding into what the Apostle Paul wanted us to receive. It is obvious that Paul was focused on bringing people into true spiritual identity.

"**Received**" in the Greek translation means to *"be in bonds, to knit together, to have obtained.* [xxi]

"Received the spirit of **adoption...**" Our adoption has given us the power to obtain. I really like the Greek word "obtain." To obtain means, "to become the possessor of" (Webster's Dictionary). We have received the power to be possessors through adoption. It is important to understand that we did not do anything to earn this honor. The cost of this privilege was not given to us, but it was paid for by the death of Jesus of Nazareth. We broke the rules and became in debt to an identity issue, and God paid for it. What a true act of the Father! Now we can say we are adopted. We have been empowered by God to **be possessors**, to obtain by our faith the proclamation that we are the **children of God**.

"*Adoption*" in the Greek means, "to bow, to commit, *to conceive*, to kneel down, to have purpose." [xxii]

Can you see how this is lining up? Our adoption has given us purpose. We are now empowered to be possessors of our purpose. Not only are we empowered to have purpose, now we are given access to possess God as our spiritual parent. God reveals His powerful intentions, to give us access to Him as beloved children. Through the Holy Spirit and through the death of Jesus, we are now spiritually and supernaturally conceived to be the sons of God. This is our right to make a powerful claim, a claim no angel in heaven can make, about God. We can say as little children "ABBA FATHER!" "DADDY GOD!" "My POPPA!"

Paul wanted to make sure that we understand not to pick up and receive the spirit of bondage; we are more than slaves or servants. We are "sons." There is no longer an Old Testament curse hanging over our heads. There is no fall of man for us to answer for. You see, in the Old Testament the high priest would only enter the Holy of Holies once a year. He was attempting at this point to reschedule judgment for the children of God. Their acts of disobedience forced them to be children of judgment. They lived under a cloud of judgment and at any moment God could rightfully and justly execute that judgment to them. Praise God! This is not for now. We are free through the blood of Jesus to boldly enter the most holy place as often as we want to without fear of judgment. Someone please shout right now, "I'm clean!"

Imagine the aggravation and exasperation the children of the Old Testament must have experienced knowing that all of their efforts would only last for one year; and that it would only work if they did the ceremonial entry exactly to the letter of the law. Can you see the burden and the fear that must have been in their hearts and minds when they entered the place of the Most High to meet Him; not as their Father, but as their God? He was not there to show them love but to make sure they obeyed the law. God loved them, but they were rebellious and sinful without any means of being cleansed, spiritually. That is the bondage and fear that Paul was speaking about.

Think about living a life without **"grace."** You would be constantly living in the fear of God's judgment, standing outside the tabernacle waiting to see if God would accept your sacrifice. Imagine attending a worship service with no guarantees that God was going to receive us. What if we had to come to church every week with that same fear? Well, we don't! Today we have a guarantee that God will receive us through the blood of Jesus, and we can receive Him as our Father. He has chosen us before we chose Him.

Praise God! You and I have not received the spirit of fear to be in bondage to the law! We have received the spirit of adoption by which we now are able to enter the most Holy Place daily, knowing that if we follow God's protocol, we can enter boldly.

"This is the covenant that I will make with them after those days, says the Lord: I will put my laws into their hearts, and in their minds I will   write them...   Their sins and their lawless deeds I will remember no more. Now where there is remission of these, there is no longer an offering for sin. Therefore, brethren, having boldness to enter into the Holiest by the blood of Jesus." Hebrews 10:16-19 NKJV

This passage has no power if we do not accept our positions in the family of God as beloved children. If we do not grasp this truth, we will not be comfortable with the fact that God wants to increase and bless everything we do. He is not judging us; He is accepting us and restoring us to our rightful place as heirs! It was never God's will for you and I to walk in sickness, lack or poverty. It was never God's intention for us to be in struggle. We are not supposed to be beat down daily by sin and circumstances. We are empowered to walk the earth as God's royal children. God destined and planned for us something much greater. Jesus called it **LIFE**! He said He came that we might have LIFE and that we might live that LIFE abundantly (John 10:10).

"But ye are a chosen generation, a royal priesthood, an holy nation, a peculiar people; that ye should shew forth the praises of him who hath called you out of darkness into his marvelous light." 1 Peter 2: 9 KJV

GENERATION NEXT!

There is a phrase that the secular world uses to express and identify what the youth of this generation should be called. They are tagged **"GENERATION X."** We are not Generation X. However, we are called **"GENERATION NEXT."**

GENERATION CHOSEN!

We are a chosen generation; chosen by God! We were handpicked and selected by Him before the foundations of the world. We were known, sanctified and ordained before we were formed. God had already planned our purpose! He spoke over us before any human on the earth ever saw us. We were appointed and set apart. Not only are we set apart, we have entered this world with the mark of blessing on us, the coat of many colors. He had already made us and strategized the plan for us before there was anything made. The Bible makes it clear that God is the "First and the Last, the Beginning and the End and the Alpha and Omega." In the Hebrew there is no word for "and." So the text actually reads that God was First, Last! Beginning, End! Alpha, Omega! When God enters first, last enters at the same time. The Word says that God knows the end from the beginning. When we see the beginning of something that God did, God has already finished it. He starts with the end and moves backwards to begin it. *Finished before started*; what POWER!

God always starts with the finished product then works His way back to the beginning. God has already been to the end of your life and worked His way back to your beginning. **God still calls you blessed** even after seeing all of your goings and comings, your ups and downs, your mistakes and failures and all of your bad decisions.

Here is the powerful truth. **We did not really choose God; God chose us**. We were incapable of finding God. First, to make the statement that we found God would insinuate that God was lost. God was not lost; we were. Second, no one could ever find God if God did not want to be found. God actually found us. We were lost, and God our Father came looking for us and made a way for us to be found. When God found us, He found us right in the middle of our stupid and our messes. Instead of judging us, Daddy God opened His arms and called us His children.

Right now would be a good place for us to stop what we are doing, lift our hands to Heaven and thank God for His mercies, His grace and His love which are new every day. Just shout it aloud. Go ahead and say it. **My Poppa, My Daddy! My Daddy GOD!**

A truly rich man is one whose children run into his arms when his hands are empty.   -- Unknown Author

CHAPTER SIX

GOD IS DEDICATED

Dedication is not what others expect of you, it is what you can give to others.

"Know therefore that the LORD thy God, he is God, the faithful God, which keepeth covenant and mercy with them that love him and keep his commandments to a thousand generations;" Deuteronomy 7:9 KJV

There are so many who have daddy issues in their lives, mainly because they have experienced an absentee daddy, or they have terrible memories of how hard and unresponsive their dad was to them. They may have had a dad who was not affectionate but overly corrective.

God is nothing like the majority of earthly fathers, and He wants us to know it. God wants us to know that as a Father, He is very different. He is clear many times in the Word that even though He is a God of laws, rules, order and principles, He is also full of mercy, grace and love. He has told us this more than a dozen times.

God is slow to anger and quick to forgive. His mercies are new every morning. He is more focused on the heart of repentance than on the infractions of our sins. To sum it up, God is a **dedicated, devoted** daddy who is always faithful!

To be **devoted** means *to be faithful, loyal, constant, and zealous in attachment.* It moves me to know that God is loyal, constant, passionate and obsessive to show me His love. God is the kind of Father that has no problem with open affections of love and shows His approval of His children deep down in places we try to hide. Isn't that what we all want from our dads?

HE WAS FAITHFUL EVEN WHEN I WAS NOT.

No matter how far we have walked away from the truths of God, no matter how rebellious we are to His ways, it is comforting to know that we never really walk away from God's love, protection and grace. God has hidden in us all of this powerful connection to Him. This connection is most revealed in times of trouble. I have witnessed people who were hard and never wanted anything to do with God. Then they experience a drastic life change. They find out they are sick or have a horrible accident. Then they call out to God. How can they do this? They know that God does not give up on us. He does not become offended with His children to the point that His anger clouds His love. How many times have our angers, hurts and offenses clouded our judgment, our decisions and our conversations? How many times have you wished you could take back something that you have said or done? It is too numerous for me to count.

There is no memory in me of any time when I came to Father God in my repentance that He made me feel shameful or disgraced in my failures. I have had many encounters of repenting for my stupid. God has always been faithful to me. He loves us even when we – His children - do not show or demonstrate that love back to Him. You must understand that it is this faithfulness that gives you and me the assurance that God the Father will not desert us or leave us. God will not kick us to the curb just because we were disobedient.

As an earthly father, I have experienced rebellious children. I have had to watch silently as my children made decisions that were contradictory to what I believe and love; drugs, sexual misconduct, ghetto mentality and so much more. They walked in darkness. I would lie in bed every night with a heavy, concerned heart. Their decisions to be stupid have been costly in so many ways, but the one thing it could not do was to change my love for them and toward them. God is not a man; He is bigger than man is. How much more is God's love toward us as His children?

NEVER RUN TOO FAR THAT YOU CANNOT RUN BACK INTO LOVE.

When the children of Israel were running from God, they seemed to always run into God. God would never give up on His children. Over and over, again and again, God would forgive them. No matter what happened, God continued to show His love through His patience. God's love is not predicated on your willingness to obey. God's love is what He is; love. He will wait on us to get it right!

What I love about God is that He will not make you follow Him or love Him first. Think about it. If God wanted to, He could make all of creation worship and adore Him regardless of what they want to do. However, that would not be real love, would it? What does it take to reveal real love? What does love do?

Love is a product of honesty, trust, and mutual respect; without these things, *you cannot have real love.*

WHAT DOES REAL LOVE LOOK LIKE?

Throughout our lives, we compile a picture of what we think real love should look like. Often this process begins early. Little girls listen to fairy tales at bedtime and envision their very own knight in shining armor. Little boys hear what princes do to rescue princesses who are in trouble. In those stories, they always use the phrase, **"true love;"** as if there is a difference between love and true love. The trouble is that the reality of love is not quite as simple as the fantasy picture we create in our heads. Our fantasy idea of love often leads us to choose romantic love instead of real love.

YOU COMPLETE ME...NOT!

After the movie Jerry McGuire, everyone started looking for a love relationship that fulfilled the phrase *"You complete me."* There is no truth in this statement. First, it says that you are not a whole person without someone else. Second, there is no human on the earth that can complete you because no human on the earth created you. To walk around looking for someone to fill your weak places is going to keep you on a search you will never complete. The only source that can complete you is God your Father. Stop looking for another to identify you, complete you or make you feel important. You must know that real love is not found by attempting to measure up to someone else. When love shows up, you will not have to do anything but receive that love with an open heart.

"Love suffers *(endures)* long and is kind *(nice, gentle, compassionate, caring, and thoughtful)*; love does not envy *(jealousy, greedy, bitter, spiteful)*; love does not parade itself, is not puffed up; does not behave rudely *(offensively, foul, crude, impolite, indecent)*, does not seek its own, is not provoked *(reactive, aggravated, annoyed, irritated, triggered)*, thinks no evil *(malicious, sinful, cruel, nasty)*; does not rejoice in iniquity *(sin, immorality, evil, injustice)*, but rejoices in the truth, bears *(tolerates, stomachs, accepts, endures)* all things, believes *(trust, considers)* all things, hopes (expectation, optimistic) all things, endures *(suffers, withstands)* all things. Love never fails *(flops, miscarries, crashes, collapses, disappoints)*. But whether there are prophecies, they will fail; whether there are tongues, they will cease; whether there is knowledge, it will vanish away." I Corinthians 13:4-8 NKJV

When there is love, there is a desire to please the one you love. What brings pleasure to the heart of a father is when his children desire to obey him. Another proof of love is **obedience**. When we desire and choose to obey God's Word, no matter what it cost, we are saying with our actions that we love God. Actions always speak louder than words.

THE DIFFERENCE BETWEEN FAVOR AND LOVE.

The difference between favor and love will be your obedience. I love my children but I bless them not according to that love but according to their obedience to my will and instructions. Yes, I do bless because of love also, but my favor is different to the obedient child verses the disobedient child.

Obedience is the prerequisite to God's best. You can have my blessing or you can have my best! When my children obey me without question, it shows me that they really love me and trust me. There is nothing more frustrating than to have your children question every command you give them. There is nothing more physically tiring than to have your instructions questioned every time you give them. I remember as a child I used to ask my father when he told me to do something, "Why?" My father would most always answer me with, **"Because I said so!"** It was not until I became a father myself that I fully

> **Obedience Is The Proof Of Real LOVE.**

understood his frustration!   Children see instructions as punishment and torture; Dads see them as training and development. The proof of a father's love is the time he takes to correct in times of failure.

Love is proven by obedience. When we obey, we are saying with actions and not just words... *I LOVE YOU, DADDY!*

Dr. Mike Murdock calls it "Hourly Obedience." Pastor Bob Weiner calls it "Instant Obedience."

OBEDIENCE IS BETTER THAN SACRIFICE.

The prophet Samuel said that obedience was better than sacrifice. No matter how you phrase it, the meaning stays the same.

- *Obedience is proof of love.*
- *Obedience is the proof of worship.*
- *Obedience is proof of respect.*

We are expressing our love when we walk in obedience. When we walk in disobedience, we are saying we just do not trust you. God's love and His father's heart prove His love when He does not cast us away or destroy us. God has true love for us!

> **OBEDIENCE IS TRUE WORSHIP! DISOBEDIENCE WILL STOP YOUR HARVEST! WALK IN HOURLY OBEDIENCE!**

We break God's heart when we choose to walk away from His goodness and love, and walk in blind disobedience. We break His heart, but He does not react to our failures and blindness with anger. He reacts with patience and love. Instead of God being angry and punishing us, HE POSITIONS HIMSELF IN A POSTURE OF WAITING ON US!

GOD'S HEART REVEALED THROUGH THE PRODIGAL SON.

In the Bible, there is a story of a man who had two sons. This father loved his sons and was dedicated to them. One day, the younger son came to his father and asked him for his inheritance early. Sons did not qualify for their inheritance until the father had passed away. You could say that the son was actually saying to his father, "Dad, I wish you were dead." The younger son revealed his orphan heart. The father was not offended and decided to give the younger son what he asked for. After receiving his inheritance, the younger son left home. The younger son did not establish a life of wealth and work with the money. The Bible says that he squandered his father's wealth. The son squandered, or misused, the money on wasteful living. Anytime we receive before we have matured, we will always waste what we get.

Why is it, as children, the minute we receive something - a word, a blessing or an answer to a question - we want to leave the place, or person, who was responsible for giving it to us? In my opinion, the biggest mistake this young man made was when he decided to leave his daddy's house.

The moment you walk out the door of your Father's house you enter into the hand of the enemy. The spirit of restlessness surrounds babes in Christ. The devil is outside the window of the house saying come on out. The minute you do, you walk away from daddy's protection. You are protected in the house. In the house, you are planted to grow. Outside the house, you will not be planted but you may be buried. There is a big difference from being planted and being buried. One has the expectation for new growth and harvest; the other has nothing but death, darkness and fear attached to it.

DEDICATED FATHER

As a father, I believe that the father in the story was deeply wounded. His mind was deeply vexed with why his son wanted to leave. When parents have to make the hard decision to let children leave, nights become sleepless and days become long and fearful. It is not so much that the son left but the way that he left. He was not sent; He went. He was following his flesh and desires that always lead to the path of wasteful living. What moves me in this story is not what the son does, but what the father does and how he reacts.

First, the father had to let him go. He did not argue with the son to stay home. The son lived a life of sin and squandered all of his father's hard saved earnings. Sin will do that to us all. *Sin will take us farther than we planned on going, keep us longer than we planned on staying and have us spend more than we planned on paying.* The result to this kind of lifestyle is exactly what happened to the young son. He became broke and bankrupt. He was living a life of lack and failure. The Bible is clear that he started working a job feeding pigs. He was doing this not just to be paid but also to eat. While he was feeding the pigs, he began to desire to eat the same food the pigs were eating. He was about to eat it and die, but God showed up. It may have been an inner thought or feeling or maybe even a voice, but what is clear is what the son heard. *"Your father's servants eat better than this."* The young man's mind was made up. *"I'll go home and at least be a servant in my daddy's house."* He was not going home to be a son, but to be a servant. This is the first sign that maturity is now finding its way into his thinking. He realized it was better to serve in his father's house than to be a slave in the devil's courts.

DISGRACED SONS ARE TO BE STONED.

The law was clear in those days. If a son disgraced the father's house, the servants would stone him for disgracing their master's house. The son was risking his life by going home; knowing that his father may not receive him and the servants may stone him. However, this was a dedicated daddy.

HEART OF THE FATHER REVEALED.

What did the father do when the younger son left? He would go out every day and look up the road confessing, believing and praying for the son's return. There is no telling how long the son was missing, but every day the **father would wait patiently.** This is a father's heart being revealed.

THE FAMILY REUNION

As I said earlier, every day the father would go and look, staring out into the empty road. He would see the shadows move as the day's sun would drift from morning to evening. Every day his heart would be so heavy until one day, the father's wish came true. That day he went out as he had done for so long and looked up that weary road. Except this day, he thought he saw something in the far distance. It looked and walked like his son and maybe, just maybe, this was his son. I imagine his son was walking slowly, thinking of how his father would respond to his return. *He probably wondered how he could face his dad. What would his dad do or say to him?* Maybe he thought, *"He may not even let me come home. I hope the servants don't stone me before I can see my father."*

The more the son walked toward his father the closer he came to being seen by the servants. He walked and the father looked, wondering was this him. He finally realizes that it is him; it was his SON!

Here is the power of the father's love. The father knew what would happen if the servants saw the rebellious son before he could do something about it. I believe one of the reasons that the father was watching for his son every day was so that *he would be the first to notice him.* The father's response touches my heart. He takes off running toward this man whom he knows is his son. He was running, shouting and when he reached his missing, lost son, the Word of God says he fell on his son's neck and cried. The daddy wrapped his loving arms around his son and said, "Welcome home, son." At the same moment the father is hugging his son, the servants were running toward this boy picking up stones as they approached him. Imagine how they felt when they got close enough to hurl those stones. To their amazement, there was the boy's daddy in the way of judgment. That is a dedicated daddy; one who is willing to risk his own life to save the life of his child. That is exactly how **Daddy God** is. **BUT WAIT, THERE IS MORE.**

This is not the end of the story. It gets even better. The father takes off his robe and places it on the young son's shoulders. The father always wants to cover his children. Then he places his signet ring on the finger of his returning son. The young son was willing to be a servant in his father's house, but the father restored to his son all that he had lost. That is the love of the father. A great father loves us and still receives us after a life of waste and loss. No matter how far we fall we can never be less than what we are, God's children. This is pure dedication, loyalty and devotion.

This is real restoration. This is exactly what you and I can expect when we come to the Father's loving arms. We get total restoration. Real love is **when you get it all back.** This makes the devil mad!   That is what a dedicated dad is like and that is exactly what **God did when He sent Jesus. God himself got in between you and judgment!**   (Luke 15:11-25)

Would you pray this prayer with me today?

Lord, help me to tap into Your love. Help me to love You and to be dedicated to You as much as You are to me. Lord, shine in my heart, as I know that I shine in Yours. Let Your liquid love flow over me.

Lord, I accept my position as Your child and with the leading of the Holy Spirit, I will be a good child.

In Jesus' Name, Amen!

CHAPTER SEVEN

GOD IS AFFECTIONATE

*"The LORD did not set his **affection** on you and choose you because you were more numerous than other peoples, for you were the fewest of all peoples. But it was because the LORD loved you and kept the oath he swore to your ancestors that he brought you out with a mighty hand and redeemed you from the land of slavery, from the power of Pharaoh king of Egypt. Know therefore that the LORD your God is God; he is the faithful God, keeping his covenant of love to a thousand generations of those who love him and keep his commandments."* Deuteronomy 7:7-9 NIV

MEN FIND IT HARD TO BE AFFECTIONATE

Most men think that because they feel love for their children, that should be enough for them to know that they love them. It is not! This is a wrong perception. You must understand how much children need their daddy to show his love with physical attention. This is the fiber that will create, in sons and daughters, a great self-image and identity. Being affectionate is not something we just do. Affection is something that is learned. Men and women who were raised in families that did not show affection may have to be taught how to show physical affection. Dads, your family needs you to show that you love them in more ways than just providing for them.

AFFECTION GUIDE:
1. Hug and kiss your wife and children, and tell them you love them daily.
2. Tell your family that you love them while you're having a meal.
3. Kiss them and tell them you love them before you leave for work.
4. Call them or text them during the day to check on them.

5. When you arrive home, make sure that you make your entrance a joy. Have a smile on your face. Hug your wife and kids. Make them feel they are the source of your joy.
6. Leave your bad day at work. Do not take it out on your family.
7. The best way for your children to know love and affection is for them to see how you treat their mom.
8. Kiss and hug your family before they go to bed.
9. Stand your kids up weekly and declare over them that they will be prosperous. Use your words as a door to their future.

Real love is not about the stuff we buy for our family. It is about the time and sacrifice we are willing to make to be with them. One Sunday morning, I was praying for a young man in his late teens. I was listening to him get his heart right with God. This young man's father was one of the wealthiest men in the church. I was thinking what could be so burdensome in his life. I could see the pain in his eyes. So I asked him, *"What's has you so torn up?"*

He looked at me and said, *"I would trade every nice thing my dad has ever bought me or did for me just to hear him say I love you or spend time with me. He's always busy!"*

Money cannot buy affection and love. Money can buy you a house but not a home. Money can buy you stuff, but it cannot buy you love. Money can buy you things, but it cannot replace time. Give your time to those you love and if you have it, then give money also.

*"Yet the LORD set his **affection** on your ancestors and loved them, and he chose you, their descendants, above all the nations-as it is today."* Deuteronomy 10:15 NIV

God, our Heavenly Father, has set His affection on us! The biggest cries from sons are they want to feel the arms of their father and his love toward them in so many ways. The truth is that children need their daddy!

Many men do not seem to understand how desperately their sons and daughters need their love, affection, approval and verbal affirmation. Sons even need a certain amount of appropriate physical touch from their dads. There is a tendency among some fathers to downplay the importance of emotion, tenderness and understanding in their interactions with their sons. I suggest, however, that this approach can be dangerous and potentially damaging. God has no problem giving us the **affection** we, as his children, need. So why should you and I?

REAL MEN DO CRY.

There is a stigma that has cursed our generation of young men for a long time. That stigma says, **"Boys aren't supposed to cry. Real men don't show their emotions."** It is ingrained in many men that masculine identity means holding back the tears except during times of extreme grief. Although women have also accepted this view, more women are voicing their belief that men and boys should be encouraged to express sensitive emotions. Crying does not make you a weak man.

What are we doing?

We are teaching our sons not to be real. We are shoving the idea down their throats that boys cannot show how they really feel. If they do, they will be tagged as **"sissies."** We are teaching our sons, who will be fathers in the next generation, that it is unnatural to hug, kiss and praise their children. If they show their feelings (sadness, crying, love or affection) they are being weak men.

I can count on one hand how many times I saw my earthly father cry while I was growing up. Now, I am not trying to make you feel like you are going to hell because you have been one of those men who could not show how you feel. However, I am trying to say that you can and should change. If God is our example, then we ought to notice that throughout the Bible, God showed His affection to His children. Again, if God the Creator does not have a problem with showing how He feels, then why should you or I?

TEARS ARE HEALTHY.

Health research has found many benefits to crying. When people suppress the urge to cry emotions, which would have been expressed through tears, are bottled up instead. The underlying biochemistry affects the body differently than if the feelings had found a physical release. Over time, repressed emotions can trigger physiological changes that manifest in clinical symptoms such as high blood pressure.

Social scientists have found correlations between men crying and their mental health. A study published in the journal *Psychology of Men & Masculinity,* found that football players who cried about game outcomes reported higher levels of self-esteem. They felt secure enough to shed tears in front of their teammates and seemed less concerned about peer pressure.[xxiii]

AFFECTION

Webster's Dictionary defines ***affectionate*** *as* *"evoking a strong emotional response, tender attachments, and fondness."*

This describes to me one of the major attributes of God as our Father. God has tender attachments to us, because we are His children.

We were made and created in His likeness according to His image. A part of all of us is also a part of God. There is a part of God that is also a part of us. His DNA connects us. The Bible says that God would **not forsake Himself.** God cannot forsake who He is. When we read that God cannot forsake Himself, I believe it is referring to us, who are made in **His image.** The verses below describe God's heart and attitude toward us, His children. Do me a favor; read the entire selection of verses and read them slowly. They are full of healing power.

"Praise the LORD, my soul; all my inmost being, praise his holy name. Praise the LORD, my soul, and forget not all his benefits- who forgives all your sins and heals all your diseases, who redeems your life from the pit and crowns you with love and compassion, who satisfies your desires with good things so that your youth is renewed like the eagle's. The LORD works righteousness and justice for all the oppressed. He made known his ways to Moses, his deeds to the people of Israel: The LORD is compassionate and gracious, slow to anger, abounding in love. He will not always accuse, nor will he harbor his anger forever; he does not treat us as our sins deserve or repay us according to our iniquities. For as high as the heavens are above the earth, so great is his love for those who fear him; as far as the east is from the west, so far has he removed our transgressions from us. As a father has compassion on his children, so the LORD has compassion on those who fear him; for he knows how we are formed, he remembers that we are dust. The life of mortals is like grass, they flourish like a flower of the field; the wind blows over it and it is gone, and its place remembers it no more. <u>But from everlasting to everlasting the LORD's love is with those who fear him, and his righteousness with their children's children-</u> with those who

keep his covenant and remember to obey his precepts."
Psalms 103:1-18 NIV

Doesn't that just show you exactly what kind of God we are serving? He is a God...

- *Who does not treat us as our sins deserve.*
- *Who does not hold His anger forever.*
- *Whose anger is for a moment.*
- *Whose love and favor are for a lifetime!*

Daddies, let me reiterate. We need to be **affectionate** with our children. We should show how we feel; we should hug them, kiss them, discipline them and play with them. By no means am I writing this with the attitude that I am or was a perfect father, or that I have arrived. Trust me; I have not! I am still fighting and wrestling with my flesh daily.

I was recently thinking about my children and how I need to be more of a disciplinarian in their lives. While I was talking to myself, I heard the still small voice of the Holy Spirit say to me. *"Discipline is a derivative of the word disciple. If you really want to be a disciplinarian in your children's lives, do what God did. Take the time to disciple them and, in the process of spending the time it takes to train them and teach them, you will be putting discipline into them."*

Too many times we think that discipline is when we are punishing our children or yelling at them to do something they do not want to do. Actually, that is the total opposite of how God has chosen to discipline us as His children.

- First, God took the time to make a plan for His children.
- Second, He took the time to train them in the plan.

GOD LOVES YOU!

God loves us with an affectionate, everlasting love!

Let's look again at the definition of the word "affectionate" and when we do, see if you do not see God *"evoking a strong emotional response, tender attachments and fondness."*

Another major inaccuracy in the Body of Christ is that we are not real when we approach God as Father. I am not saying that we are not real in what we feel in our approach but that we are not real in how we act after we have entered His presence. Why is it when people pray they sound different? They act different? God knows who you are before you entered His presence. There is nothing hidden from His eyes. His love has given us access that no other generation had in the Old Testament. We can do, and are allowed to do, what angels themselves cannot do. We can enter boldly. We can enter confidently. We can enter, not as sinners, not as servants, but as sons. I may have a servant's heart, but I have a son's mentality.

The one thing I want as a father is for my children to be real in my presence; not real as in the fact that they do not know their place as children and not real in that they disrespect me. I want them to be genuine. There is a difference in being real and being dishonorable. They should know that I am love, but also I have order. Enter my atmosphere with order and you will

> **A Servant's Heart; A Son's Mentality.**

always get my attention. I want them to know who I am as their father and to be real with me as my children. I want my children to tell me what is bothering them, what is hurting them and what arouses their curiosity. *God the Father is the same.*

When we enter the Father's presence, we need to learn to be real. When we are real, we are being authentic, genuine and true. What God wants us to do is to be real.

- *What is moving you will move God.*
- *What excites you-your dreams, goals and visions-will excite God.*
- *He is moved and touched by our feelings.*

"For we have not an high priest which cannot be touched with the feeling of our infirmities; but was in all points tempted like as we are, yet without sin." Hebrews 4:15 KJV

God can be affected, impressed, moved and touched. There is the difference! **GOD is real!** God is not a God who does not want to be touched. He desires to feel what we feel.

PROTOCOL IS IMPORTANT.

Even though God gives us access there are rules, procedures and policies we must not cross. Breaking protocol can be very costly, if not dangerous.

We must always keep in mind that God is supreme and all-powerful, and He is our Father. Never get it twisted. *God is not human!* <u>God is not a man</u> (Numbers 23:19)! **He is God!** When we approach Him, we must always be mindful that God is a Spirit. He is not flesh. We are allowed access; we are not demanding it. God has invited us into a relationship that no other creature is privileged to have. We can enter boldly! We can stay in His presence as long as we stay in the spirit. Our access is pure FAVOR! God consents Himself the freedom to be touched. This is where connection is powerful. What an awesome, loving Daddy God He is!

TURN THE HEARTS TO THE FATHER.

"And he will go on before the Lord, in the spirit and power of Elijah, to turn the hearts of the parents to their children and the disobedient to the wisdom of the righteous-to make ready a people prepared for the Lord." Luke 1:17 NIV (Note: This a direct quote found also in the book of Malachi as shown below.)

"See, I will send you the prophet Elijah before that great and dreadful day of the LORD comes. He will turn the hearts of the parents to their children, and the hearts of the children to their parents; or else I will come and strike the land with total destruction." Malachi 4:5-6 NIV

It is interesting to me that one of the last words spoken by the Lord in the Old Testament was, *"**He will turn the hearts of the fathers to their children, and the hearts of the children to their fathers..."(KJV).*** Many have made the book of Malachi all about the tithe, but the real focus is **honor!**

God was questioning their honor and loyalty. The proof of dishonor was in their giving. Real love and honor always want to give the best gifts. When we hold back our giving, we are expressing that we love another. We honor another. We honor our kids more than we honor God. We honor our jobs more than we honor God. We honor ourselves more than we honor God. Wherever your money is, so is your heart. *"For where your treasure is, there your heart will be also"* (Matthew 6:21). In this book about honor, the last words of Malachi are about turning the hearts of the father and the children back to each other.

God wanted us to know that one of the whole reasons for sending Jesus was to mend the heart of the children so that they could fulfill the heart of the fathers. Now, in the natural we think of the families that are messed up due to divorce and other attacks.

Studying these verses, I was moved in my spirit to look deeper into them. After a moment of thinking, I saw what the Holy Spirit was trying to paint in my imagination. This scripture is not just for the earthly fathers, it was also written as the description of the heart and affection of God as our Father.

God the Father was going to turn the wicked, lost and rebellious child's heart back toward Him as Father. God was going to turn the heart of stone in his children back to a heart of flesh. He was going to do this through His son, Jesus. His love for all cost Him His love for the One. Not only was God giving with such love but he also was paying for what He already owned. Not only was God the Father mending the hearts of the children, He was also mending **the gap** that was in His heart from their heart.

God Loves YOU So Much!

REAL LOVE!

There were 400 years of silence between the book of Malachi and the book of Matthew. Even though God was silent, He didn't leave them without a promise to look forward to. The hearts of sons would return to the heart of the fathers. God would also mend the heart of the fathers, and that heart was the heart that was in God toward His children.

GOD LOVES FAMILY!

God has spared no expense, time or words to show you and me that He is a dedicated, devoted and affectionate Father!

Take a moment and really consider how you got

saved. Be truthful! Remember, no one has ever really found God. God has never been lost! God could never get lost, **He's God! God found us**

We were lost! We were the ones who needed to be found. Like most, I was not looking to be found. I did not know how dark my world was; not until I found Jesus and He introduced me to the Father. The Father sent down His Spirit to enter me. Up until that day, I was too busy attempting to live life without a Heavenly Father. So what really happened? **God found me!**

The Father came looking for us and found us. What did He find? He found us in a mess, living a wasteful life, just like the prodigal son. Somewhere in the midst of my mess, God sent His Word to remind me of His home where He was waiting for me. So in the end, God found us while we were still wicked and deceived. We were incapable of finding God. **Therefore, God found us!**

"The human spirit is the lamp of the Lord that sheds light on one's inmost being." Proverbs 20:27 NIV

"Yet a time is coming and has now come when the true worshipers will worship the Father in the Spirit and in truth, for they are the kind of worshipers the Father seeks." John 4:23 NIV

"The LORD regretted that he had made human beings on the earth, and his heart was deeply troubled." Genesis 6:6 NIV

"And they put away the strange gods from among them, and served the LORD: and his soul was grieved for the misery of Israel." Judges 10:16 KJV

"He looked around at them <u>in anger</u> and, <u>deeply distressed</u> at their stubborn hearts, said to the man, "Stretch out your hand." He stretched it out, and his hand was completely restored." Mark 3:5 NIV

"And do not <u>grieve the Holy Spirit of God</u>, with whom you were sealed for the day of redemption." Ephesians 4:30 NIV

"As a father pities his children, so the Lord pities those who fear Him. For He knows our frame; He remembers that we are dust." Psalms 103:13-14 NKJV

CHAPTER EIGHT

GOD IS DETERMINED

Determined is defined as decided and resolved, to fix conclusively or authoritatively. *(Webster's Dictionary)*

We must take an expedition back in time to fully understand what it means for God to be determined. We need to go back to the book of Genesis in the first chapter, way back to the beginning before there was anything. God paid a high price for us to have a relationship with Him, but why?

WAS GOD LONELY?

I am not talking about lonely in the way you and I think of being lonely. First of all, God was not alone. God had angels that worshipped Him, took care of Him and guarded His very presence. Secondly, I do not believe that God was uncomfortable being by himself, feeling isolated or not "feeling" loved.

However, God had no one around Him that He allowed to know Him. Angels obey Him. Angels fear Him. Angels carry out His will; but they do not have the right to know Him.

God was not alone, but He was secluded in that He needed to create true love. True love is different. True love has to have freedom attached to it; freedom to leave or stay and freedom to obey or disobey. God, in His supreme power, could make everything love him, but if I make you love me then how do I know you really love me?

To know if you love me, I have to show you what I wish and desire of you and allow you to choose. If you choose to do what I ask, then you have proven in your will that you love me.

God knew that when He opened that box He would have to have to live with the pain of loving someone who did not love Him back. I have experienced this in a small way with my own children; loving them so deeply while watching them make choices that I will have to pull them out of and rescue them from total defeat in the end.

GOD DECIDED TO MAKE A FAMILY.

First, God had to build an environment for His family to live in and raise his family in. God had to establish an atmosphere that His family could exist in. He had to make a man and then make woman from the man.

THE BEGINNINGS

God created the earth. Then He created living creatures. Next he formed and birthed man, Adam, from the earth. He then pulled Eve out of Adam. Then God made a garden called Eden. Eden would be the atmosphere where He could shelter and enjoy His son and raise His family. So then, God had to establish a test so that man could prove their love through faithfulness.

The proof of love is when you can exist in the house and obey the boundaries and rules of the house. The Father sets up guidelines places them in the house called Eden; boundaries that were not to be crossed.

I have been married for twenty-seven years, and there are certain things I know I need not do in my marriage. If I break certain boundaries or rules it could cost me my marriage. It could break up our unity. My love for my wife causes me to submit to her wishes, to her guidelines. I dare not cross them for fear of losing what I love.

MAN IS A MYSTERY.

God created the perfect environment, **"Eden"**. In Eden He set up the parameters of how large this environment would be. He put all the right plants and animals in this environment. After God completed His garden, He was ready for His greatest achievement, man. Even the Angels had a hard time understanding man.

*"It is not to angels that he has subjected the world to come, about which we are speaking. But there is a place where someone has testified: **What is mankind that you are mindful of them, a son of man that you care for him?** You made him a little lower than the angels; you crowned them with glory and honor and put everything under their feet."*
Hebrews 2:5-8 NIV

God created a perfect place where the atmosphere was conducive to His presence (Eden). God placed man in this Eden. Man is not just some ordinary creature. Man is God's masterpiece! This is the greatest of all of God's doings. Man was formed out of dirt. God made land before He made man. God put in the land all the prosperity that is on the land. Gold, diamonds, oil, precious stones and so much more all come from the land. God made man from land. Land became man! All the prosperity in the land, and more, is in man. God put His spirit in man. God's seed is in man.

"So God created mankind in his own image, in the image of God he created them; male and female he created them."
Genesis 1:27 NIV

All children are the harvest of their father's seed. They have their individuality, but they also have their identity. That identity was engrafted in the father's seed that is part of the make and fiber of the children. *Are you catching the emphasis of this entire garden creation?*

Right in the middle of this picture-perfect world, God planted two important trees. One was called the tree of life; the other was called the tree of the knowledge of good and evil. The test! The proof of man's love was in the midst of these trees!

"Now the LORD God had planted a garden in the east, in Eden; and there he put the man he had formed. The LORD

God made all kinds of trees grow out of the ground--trees that were pleasing to the eye and good for food. In the middle of the garden were <u>the tree of life</u> and <u>the tree of the knowledge of good and evil.</u> " Gen 2:8-9 NIV

THE REQUEST: COMMAND

God gave instructions to Adam. He said, *"Eat of anything you wish in this garden except one tree is forbidden...* the **'tree of the knowledge of good and evil.'**
- Do not look at it.
- Do not touch it.
- Do not eat it.

The rules were clear and the consequence was established; *"the day you do eat of it you will surely die."* Notice, God did not say He would kill them. He said they would die. So why after they disobeyed did they not die? The moment they disobeyed, they began to deteriorate. God's breath ceased to breathe in them that day. Isn't that what it means to die; to stop breathing? If they disobeyed, they would die, but as long as they focused on and ate from the tree of life, they would never die. That tree was life! It was God's established Word. When we partake of God's Word, it brings us life. When we ignore it, it brings us death.

The Word of God has two parts – Revelation and Knowledge. If you seek revelation and stay focused on Jesus, you will walk in obedience. If you seek knowledge, you will be responsible for the knowledge you possess. Jesus is LIFE! Knowledge is DEATH! Knowledge requires tests. Tests reveal what knowledge you possess.

Obedience to God's Word qualifies us to live in God's Eden. The Word is the only way God can test our true love. Adam broke the Words of God and rebelled against the instruction, "Do not eat from the tree of the knowledge of good and evil…"

THE ANATOMY OF LOSS

Every day God would reveal Himself and enter Eden to walk and fellowship with the man that was made in His image. When we obey God's wishes, we always walk with God's favor.

I can imagine that God would appear and Adam would be waiting. One evening God appeared and man was not waiting. Man was not eager to see God. For the first time God had to walk around His garden looking for man. Man was lost. Where was man? He was hiding in the bushes. Why was he hiding? Man could hear the voice of God, but now that voice was law, not love. Adam's disobedience had blocked the love voice. Adam did not understand this new sound. When God found him, He asked Adam, ***"Why are you hiding from me?"***

Adam said, *"God, did you know we are naked! We are not really like you; we are human. God, we are flesh and blood, we are not spirit!"*

God was disturbed and in His response, we can see His brokenness. *"Adam, who told you that you were naked. You did not eat from the tree of knowledge did you?* ***Oh, Adam! Please tell me you did not ruin what we have.*** You didn't disobey me?" Adam said, "Oh God, it's the woman you gave me."

> **A Broken Heart, A Loving Father**

God turned to Eve and said, "Eve, what have you done?" You can hear the disappointment in those words. God knew the ramifications of what was about to happen, just like we do as parents when we watch our children rebel against the rules.

Eve pointed to the serpent, "God the serpent beguiled me..."

GOD STAYS CONNECTED

Man rejected the Truth, but the Truth did not reject mankind. After man openly walked in disobedience, God would not forsake His creation. What did God do? God provided a way of escape. God killed innocent animals and made a tunic of skin to cloth their nakedness; a covering by the shedding of blood. God had already established what it was going to take to redeem mankind. The phrase *"mankind"* does not appear in the Bible until after the fall. The word always said man. After the fall, Adam became a different "kind" of man! **Redemption** is now the new focus of the Kingdom of God.

"Then the eyes of both of them were opened, and they realized they were naked; so they sewed fig leaves together and made coverings for themselves." Genesis 3:7 NIV

Get a clear picture in your mind. God stood there and allowed his children to leave His garden knowing what they were going to face. They had to leave the safety of His presence. They left the comfort of His prosperity to live among the laws of sowing and reaping. They would have to experience lies, deceit, pain, loss and eventually death. I can see the heart of God being broken and saddened; not because He had lost something but because He knew what man had lost. They lost the best thing that was going for them. They lost access to the Father! The Father had now become their God. Believe me, there is a difference. Now, they would take on the "orphan" image. Self-Awareness became the focus of men.

God shares with man what He knows. The woman

will now have to suffer great travail in birth. The ground is cursed and man will have to work to reverse the curse of the ground. Through man's sweat, they will now provide food. God did not let the serpent off the hook either. God said something that gives us the whole plan. Satan did not surprise God one minute. God knew that the enemy would challenge His creation. This time, when there was an infraction, there would be a way of escape for His children.

"So the LORD God said to the serpent, "Because you have done this, Cursed are you above all livestock and all wild animals! You will crawl on your belly and you will eat dust all the days of your life. And I will put enmity between you and the woman, and between your offspring and hers; he will crush your head, and you will strike his heel."
Genesis 3:14-15 NIV

IT WAS A SET UP!

God set the devil up. Satan must have assumed that woman was weaker than man was so He deceived her first. God designed His plan around the womb of a woman. He was going to sow His seed and produce another kind of man, a God man (Jesus). Adam and Eve attempted to cover their sins. Here is where we see the first glimmer of religion. Religion is always the attempt to cover up to stay connected. Religion masks what we are really like, and it hides what needs to be revealed to God.

God reached down, grabbed innocent animals, tore the skin right off their bodies and sewed together a tunic. The word tunic in the Hebrew gives us the clarity of God's action. Tunic means **"propitiation,** a covering; not a cover up!" Imagine how much blood was on the ground that day. The one thing that Adam and Eve knew when they were exiting Eden was that *without the shedding of blood there would be* *no remission of sins.*

Here we witness God's willpower, His resolve and His dedication. God began His long process to escort His children back and to bridge the gap in His heart.

God could have been completely different. He could have just erased it all and started over, but that would not have been real love. Real love takes the good times with the bad times. Real love will pick up the broken pieces and find a way to put them back together.

God took the pain and committed to redeem His man, or mankind. Today, we are the testimony of His affectionate, devoted and determined love. Remember our definition of determined...*"To fix conclusively and authoritatively."* God, through Jesus, repaired the problem conclusively. There is no dispute in that Jesus redeemed us and placed the favor of God upon us by his shed blood. We have overcome the devil by the blood of the Lamb and by the words of our testimony.

"They triumphed over him by the blood of the Lamb and by the word of their testimony; they did not love their lives so much as to shrink from death." Revelation 12:11 NIV

JESUS IS THE UNDISPUTED CHAMPION!

God does not just forgive us. He redeems us! Redeem is a banking term. It means to exchange, to buy back, to recover, to release, to liberate and to emancipate. Through Jesus' death on the cross, He became the payment, the exchange. Through His resurrection from the dead, He became the release and emancipator from the curse. God gave Jesus all authority in Heaven and on the Earth. What did Jesus do with all that authority and power? Jesus gave that authority and power to His church. Who is that? *That is you and me!* Not only did God repair the problem, He also gave us **power over the problem** by the Spirit of the Word.

"In whom we have redemption, the forgiveness of sins.
The Son is the image of the invisible God, the firstborn over
all creation. For in him all things were created: things in
heaven and on earth, visible and invisible, whether thrones
or powers or rulers or authorities; all things have been
created through him and for him. He is before all things, and
in him all things hold together. And he is the head of the
body, the church; he is the beginning and the firstborn from
among the dead, so that in everything he might have the
supremacy. For God was pleased to have all his fullness
dwell in him, and through him to reconcile to himself all
things, whether things on earth or things in heaven, by
making peace through his blood, shed on the cross."
Colossians 1:14-20 NIV

CHAPTER NINE

YOU WILL NOT BE DENIED

*"For all the promises of God in him are yea, and in him
Amen, unto the glory of God by us."*
2 Corinthians 1:20

*"We are troubled on every side, yet not distressed; we are
perplexed, but not in despair; Persecuted, but not forsaken;
cast down, but not destroyed."*
2 Corinthians 4:8-9

Covenant means nothing if you do not know what is in the covenant. Birthright means nothing if you do not know whom your father is. I want to open to you the storehouse of your birthright, the importance of knowing your spiritual legacy. Believers all over the church are missing this one important concept of God being their Father. Because He is our Father, He wants to bless us in every good way. What is your birthright? Prosperity is your birthright. I know that prosperity gets a lot of negative publicity in the church. I do not understand the hostility toward spiritual prosperity.

The most celebrated demon in hell is the one that was sent to tell you God wants you poor! I hear people who have been saved for some time say, **"I'm tired of hearing about money in the church."** To me, this is the most stupid and ignorant statement anyone could ever make. Money should be spoken about in church every week. Jesus spoke more about money than He did Heaven or Hell. Money is the smallest part of God's treasures. However, money is the test to unlock all of His blessings. The gold of Heaven is attached to your response and use of money. What do you do with it? How do you sow it? How does it make you feel? If you hate prosperity, you are going to be the most miserable person in Heaven, assuming you

> **Wealth is Bigger Than Money!**

even make it. Seriously, I cannot think of a better place to talk about money than in the house of God. Satan does not fear our praise. He is not intimidated with our preaching. Satan has no worries about evangelism as long as you have no prosperity. You want to see "warfare?" Start teaching people to walk in prosperity and watch how many attacks begin to show up. The truth is that without prosperity you are weak and powerless in a world that runs on money. Money decides influence. Money pays for vision. Money feeds the hungry. Money is not evil. Money is merely a tool. In the right hands, it becomes a weapon for the righteous; in the wrong hands, it becomes a weapon against the righteous.

How can anyone who reads and studies the Word of God miss the whole message of the Gospel? Yes, I said the whole message of the Gospel. Prosperity is the Gospel. Without it, we cannot preach a message of restoration.

The birthright gives me the access to increase in every area of my life. My inheritance is attached to my birthright. As long as we live like orphans in the church, we are saved with no connection to our Daddy. Daddy God is bigger than money. God is the God of wealth. Wealth is more than just money; wealth is when you have enough harvest (money) for yourself and for others who are in need. God is a God of wealth, but we struggle with the word prosperity. We are full of "Christians" in the House of God who cannot even pay their utility bill. Forty-Five percent of all bankruptcy happens within the church. We fight the very word that could liberate us from bondage. Jesus came to make men free. You are not truly free until you are debt free. You will never be debt free if you have no prosperity. You will never have prosperity until you know your birthright. Our birthright is that we are children of God and because we are God's children, we walk in supernatural wealth.

*"A feast is made for laughter, and wine makes life merry, **and money is the answer for everything."** Ecclesiastes 10:19 NIV

- If you desire to keep your house or car, you will have to keep giving the Mortgage Company or creditor your money.
- If you want to buy new clothes, you will have to give the department store your money.

- If we need to build a gymnasium or a youth room to reach young people, it will take our **money to do it**.
- If you desire to help feed the hungry, it will take your money to buy the food to feed them.
- The whole world works around money.
- If increase is wrong and ungodly then why do we accept promotions and pay raises?

We really do not believe that money is evil or increase is wrong. We just do not want to equate money with sowing and reaping. We do not want to attach our increase and blessing to God. As long as our money comes from our own efforts, we are fine. We have placed no significance on God. There is no responsibility for it. The moment we make God *our source* we begin to squirm. We do not want God to be the reason for our increase because it puts us responsible to God. The truth is we only want to be responsible to ourselves.

This is not contrary to the Word of God; this is a direct order of the Word of God.

"So you are no longer a slave, but God's child; and since you are his child, God has made you also an heir." Galatians 4:7 NIV

The word heir in this scripture signifies you have a birthright. God has made us His beneficiaries. But what is an heir? Let's take a closer look at this verse, and we will qualify the rest of it in context.

The Greek word for heir is *kleronomos (klay-ron-om'-os);* which means a **sharer by lot,** i.e. **inheritor** (literally or figuratively); by **implication, a possessor**: by implication a portion, a patrimony, figuratively); KJV - heritage, inheritance, lot, part.[xxiv]

Paul is teaching us that we have a partnership through inheritance. If we do not read this passage in context, we will miss the partnership. Let's go to the beginning of this chapter and look at it in its entirety.

*"What I am saying is that as long as **an heir** is **underage**, he is **no different from a slave**, although he owns the whole estate. The heir is subject **to guardians and trustees until the time set by his father**. So also, when we were underage, we were in slavery under the elemental spiritual forces of the world. But when the set time had fully come, God sent his Son, born of a woman, born under law, **to redeem those under law**, that we might receive **adoption to sonship**. Because you are his sons, God sent the Spirit of his Son into our hearts, the Spirit who calls out, **"Abba, Father."** So you are no longer a slave, but **God's child**; and since you are his **child**, God has made you **also an heir**."* Galatians 4:1-7 NIV

Children are slaves to the laws of parents. As long as we remain a child in the Kingdom, we will not be released to full maturity. We will only live on what we have and not what has been set up through promise. As long as we cling to the basic milk of God's Word, we will remain a slave. When did God call Jesus His son? When Jesus turned thirty years old. Jesus stopped being a child and started walking in "sonship" Then all rights were fully bestowed to Him.

When my son was 11-years-old, he had an obsession and love for knives and guns. What if I gave my son a loaded gun and sent him off to school, but told him before he left the house that this weapon was only for his protection. I know what you are thinking. No daddy in his right mind would give his 11-year-old son a real loaded handgun. Of course, you are right!

Let's say that my eleven-year-old son asked me for a thousand dollars. I could give it to him, but would I? No, I would not. Why? Because an eleven year old cannot handle $1,000.00. As his father, I want to train him and raise him so that when he becomes a fully mature man he can have more than what I have. He would move from under my guardianship to fully mature. He qualifies for all my rights and wealth.

This is exactly what Paul is trying to teach us in Galatians. *If the son is a child, he is no different from a slave.* He will always be under the control of a guardian. He may own everything in the house, but the father is not going to release what is rightfully his until he is mature enough to handle it. That means the father trusts the son not to waste the blessing.

The church has been sitting in spiritual slavery because it will not come into full maturity. The people will not try to mature past water baptism, salvation and going to heaven. If we continue to walk this path and ignore growing up on the meat of God's Word, we will live constantly at the mercy of our enemies. If we stay only focused on the elementary teachings of the Word of God we will never take our place as sons and daughters of God. Imagine what we could do as believers if we would step out of "immature thinking" and start walking in full maturity in the Lord.

"But when the time had fully come..."

Time has fully come. The word "fully" here in the Greek means abundantly. When time came full circle and once again became qualified for abundance, God sent His son, Jesus. God sent Him to redeem those who are under the law so that we could walk in full rights as children (sons). Notice, to receive what is **rightfully ours**; God wants us to become obsessed with what belongs to us by birthright! Do you enter your own home through permission of someone else? Do you have to ask if you want something to eat? Do you have to pray about what to wear? Do you seek God when you are ready to get in your car and drive somewhere? No; absolutely not, because all of those things are rightfully yours. When you keep asking God for things that through maturity you should know are yours, God cannot give them to you because it would be affirming wrong behavior and wrong identity. Do you understand what I am saying?

Believe It to Receive It! Doubt it; Do Without It!

When we believe that God wants to meet our needs, we are actually pleasing Him. No good daddy would not want to give His children the best he has. There will never be a day in my children's lives that if they needed me I would not desire to meet their needs according to my riches, not theirs. That is just what God wants us to get. If we ask, and if we believe, we **will not be denied! Believe it and receive it...doubt it and do without it.**

All of God's promises are yes and amen!

"BIRTHRIGHT"

Webster's Dictionary defines **"birthright"** as a right, or the rights that a person has because of being born in a certain family, nation, etc.

Do not let a moment of desire rob you from a lifetime of blessing!
There is a story in the Bible that shows what can happen when you do not fully understand the power of a birthright!

"Once when Jacob was cooking some stew, Esau came in from the open country, famished. He said to Jacob, 'Quick,

let me have some of that red stew!   I'm famished!' (That is why he was also called Edom.) Jacob replied, 'First sell me your birthright.' 'Look, I am about to die,' Esau said. 'What good is the birthright to me?' But Jacob said, 'Swear to me first.' So he swore an oath to him, selling his birthright to Jacob. Then Jacob gave Esau some bread and some lentil stew. He ate and drank, and then got up and left.
So Esau despised his birthright." Genesis 25:29-34 NIV

Jacob's name alone tells us who he is in the story. His name in the Hebrew means "heel," or "trickster." Here comes Esau. He is famished and desires something to fill his obsession for food. He has a craving for what he smells cooking in the kitchen.

Esau is a type of the church. The church is full of Esau's people who have cravings for things and will do whatever it takes to satisfy those cravings before thinking through the consequences.

Jacob says, "I'll give you what you want, but before I do sell me your birthright!"

Esau had a moment-to-moment need. If he would have not been lazy and tired, he could have taken the time necessary and prepared himself a meal. Instead, he let his immediate need dictate his future demise.

Esau is no different than most of the saints today in our churches. People come into the house of God with so many attractions, distractions and immediate needs that they cannot see past their own hunger and cravings.

They sit, week after week, and become angry and mad at the preacher. They become mad at God and mad at everyone around them because they are famished. They are famished and craving things that will only satisfy the moment. People are giving up their birthright for comfort and convenience. Instead of opening up the bread of heaven and eating from the Word of God, they just sit and wait for the

Jacob spirit to come and deceive them into selling their **birthright** for an immediate fix.

Think of how many church-going people sell their birthright to satisfy an immediate need. The twenty first century church is so caught up in the mentality of 'instant and now,' that Satan does not have to work hard at deceiving the people of God into giving up their birthrights. When you walk away from your birthright, you are saved with no provision. You will have vision, but you will not have provision!

What did Esau take for his birthright? A bowl of soup! Now if that does not seem ignorant to you than God help you. This man had the right to everything His daddy, Isaac, owned. Isaac is a type of **Daddy God**! God is only going to bless those who have and walk in the birthright.

Stop allowing the enemy, or anyone else, to rob you of your right to be blessed. If you understand your birthright, you will walk up to your heavenly Father and God will not deny you what is rightfully yours by spiritual birth. **You will not be denied!** God is not going to turn away the children who hold the **birthright**. That **birthright** for you and me is faith in the Lord. It is the understanding of God and His desire to bless His children. It is not receiving the spirit of fear, but the spirit of *adoption* by which we cry out "ABBA FATHER," Daddy God!

So many in our churches are like Esau. Esau tried to get Isaac to bless him and even told Isaac that Jacob tricked him. Isaac could not do anything to help Esau, for once the hand of blessing was passed there was no retracting it. *What God blesses no one can curse.* The good news here is that if we walk according to the **Word of God,** we are then the children of God. God calls us blessed! What God blesses, no one or anything can stop us from that blessing! The only thing that can stop us from receiving our blessing is if we make wrong decisions to fulfill fleshly passions. Then we would sell our birthright to satisfy the instant.

Esau said, "Isn't he rightly named Jacob? This is the second time he has taken advantage of me: He took my birthright, and now he's taken my blessing!" Then he asked, "Haven't you reserved any blessing for me?" Gen 27:36 NIV

Please learn the lesson early! The more we sit in our churches and want to be instantly satisfied, the more we will eventually sell out to the wrong spirit.

We must realize that the Christian walk is a process. It is a process before it is position. It takes time for things to change. The fruit of those who are sitting in your churches, those with the Esau spirit, will always be dissatisfied with the leaders that God has placed over them. They will always complain about everything. Nothing will ever be good enough. The music will either be too spiritual or not be spiritual enough. The pastor will never preach good enough; the service will never be spiritual enough; the prayer groups do not know how to pray; the staff does not have the right attitude to be paid. There will always be something to complain about in the heart of an Esau.

SIGNS THAT YOU HAVE AN ESAU SPIRIT:

- Restlessness
- Confusion
- Worry
- An unquenchable thirst for instant gratification.

Avoid these kinds of people; they will eventually sell their birthright. If you are not careful, you will end up following them and giving up yours, too. Do not let the complainers rob you of your right to be blessed! Remember, if you are walking according to God's Word, **you will not be denied** because you are the children of God!

CHAPTER TEN

BE A GOOD STEWARD

Please take the time to read these verses slowly and listen to the Spirit of God.

"Again, it will be like a man going on a journey, who called his servants and entrusted his wealth to them. To one he gave five bags of gold, to another two bags, and to another one bag, each according to his ability. Then he went on his journey. The man who had received five bags of gold went at once and put his money to work and gained five bags more. So also, the one with the two bags of gold gained two more. But the man who had received one bag went off, dug a hole in the ground and hid his master's money. After a long time the master of those servants returned and settled accounts with them. The man who had received five bags of gold brought the other five. 'Master,' he said, 'you entrusted me with five bags of gold. See, I have gained five more.' His master replied, 'Well done, good and faithful servant! You have been faithful with a few things; I will put you in charge of many things. Come and share your master's happiness!' The man with the two bags of gold also came. 'Master,' he said, 'you entrusted me with two bags of gold; see, I have gained two more.' His master replied, 'Well-done, good and faithful servant! You have been faithful with a few things; I will put you in charge of many things. Come and share your master's happiness!' Then the man who had received one bag of gold came. 'Master,' he said, 'I knew that you are a hard man, harvesting where you have not sown and gathering where you have not scattered seed. So I was afraid and went out and hid your gold in the ground. See, here is what belongs to you.' His master replied, 'You wicked, lazy servant! So you knew that I harvest where I have not sown and gather where I have not scattered seed? Well then, you should have put my money on deposit with the bankers, so that when I returned I would have received it back with interest. So take the bag of gold from him and give it to the

one who has the ten bags. For whoever has will be given more, and they will have an abundance. Whoever does not have, even what they have will be taken from them. And throw that worthless servant outside, into the darkness, where there will be weeping and gnashing of teeth.' When the Son of Man comes in his glory, and all the angels with him, he will sit on his glorious throne. All the nations will be gathered before him, and he will separate the people one from another as a shepherd separates the sheep from the goats. He will put the sheep on his right and the goats on his left. Then the King will say to those on his right, 'Come, you who are blessed by my Father; take your inheritance, the kingdom prepared for you since the creation of the world."
Matthew 25:14-34 NIV

I strategically put this here because you must know that if you are not a good steward of what you have been given, God will not give you any more. What are the keys to these verses? First, the master gave all of them enough to increase. Second, the master did not demand that they all increase at the same level. They were to increase at the level they were blessed. Third, they were required to do whatever it took to increase.

The one with five bags of gold increased five more bags, and the one with two bags increased two more bags. The one with one bag of gold hid it.

The bag of gold could represent many things. It could represent gifts or money. I believe its money. We are walking opposite to the plan and law of God when we choose to hide what God gave us. Fear is one of the reasons people hide what has been given to them. Fear is a reason people will not give; fear is a paralyzing force in the body of Christ.

The master came to settle the accounts. When he inquired of the one 'bag of gold' person's record he replied, *"I was afraid and hid my money. Here master, I have kept it and no one has ever used it or touched it. It is exactly the way you gave it to me." (Paraphrased)* This angered the master! He did not give the money for it to stay the same. He gave it to be increased and enjoy a life without fear and worry. Instead, the man lived his whole life in the religion of mediocrity. He did just enough to get by. He took what was given to him and wasted the time granted to increase. This is the attitude of the majority of God's children; mediocrity in everything we do. Mediocrity in our attendance, in our giving, in our praise, in our worship, in our witness, in our passion, in our relationships and our vocation; just doing enough to get by. How can we be so blind? God the Father gave us a most precious gift and that gift is to increase. We take that gift, put it in the dirt and hide it.

Watch the response of the master here…

"You wicked and lazy servant, you knew that I was going to expect a return from my investment. You said it out of your own mouth." (Paraphrased)

The master did not just rebuke him. He took the bag from him, gave it to the one with ten bags, and told him to walk in abundance.
Abundance is when you receive increase, and you did not even have to work for it. The man with ten bags of gold increased by the master's hand because he was faithful with what he had in his hand.
Right now would be a good place for you to shout, *"Thank you, God!"* God is going to bless us because we are faithful with what we have. Increase is the way of the Word of God. Do not let someone put condemnation on you because you desire to better yourself. In fact, move away from anyone who doesn't want to increase. Run as fast as you can from the spirit of **mediocrity!**

Laziness has consequences attached to it.

Look at the anger in the master's voice and attitude…
"Take this worthless servant and throw him outside into the darkness, where there will be weeping and gnashing of teeth" (Paraphrased). **This is HELL!**

The master sent this servant to hell, not because he was sleeping around, not because he was rebellious, not even because he was a hater of God. No, he threw him in **HELL** because he was lazy, took the gift, and hid it. He did not affect or change anything or anyone around him. He just sat in church logging time on the spiritual clock, singing the songs and acting as if he was a lover of God. In reality, he was lazy and never helped anyone else find the Lord. God was so angry that He put him in hell!

The conclusion of the story…

"For I was hungry and you gave me something to eat, I was thirsty and you gave me something to drink, I was a stranger and you invited me in, I needed clothes and you clothed me, I was sick and you looked after me, I was in prison and you came to visit me.' Then the righteous will answer him, 'Lord, when did we see you hungry and feed you, or thirsty and give you something to drink? When did we see you a stranger and invite you in, or needing clothes and clothe you? When did we see you sick or in prison and go to visit you?' He will reply, 'Truly I tell you, whatever you did not do for one of the least of these, you did not do for me.' Then they will go away to eternal punishment, but the righteous to eternal life."
Matthew 25:35-41 NIV

Jesus is coming back one day to gather all of Daddy's children. Let's pray right now that we will be considered sheep and not goats.

THERE IS A DIFFERENCE BETWEEN SHEEP AND GOATS

Sheep will only eat one thing and that will be what the shepherd has approved; good green pastures. Goats will eat anything! Goats will eat garbage, and when there is nothing left to eat, they will bite each other.

Sheep gather in flocks and are led by a shepherd. Goats are loners and cannot be led by anyone. Sheep are compliant, and goats are rebellious. Sheep are shy and peaceful, and goats are arrogant and loud.

Let's not be goats. We will never do anything for God in our churches if we keep allowing the goats to take over! Goats want nothing to do with change and increase.

Daddy God wants us to be children who believe it is possible to change and increase, not because of man's abilities, but because we believe in our birthright. The birthright says, "I have the right to **INCREASE**! I will not be denied what is rightfully mine."

Pray this prayer with me right now:

Lord, I confess that without You I am nothing. Lord, I want to be a vessel of honor to You and ask that right now you begin to change the way I think and act.

Lord, come into my atmosphere and take control of what is around me. If there is anything in my life that is causing a hindrance and keeping me from Your best, You have my permission to remove it.

I love You and want to increase. I rebuke, in the name of Jesus, all thoughts that try to sway me against the prosperity message. Lord, help me to be a blessing to others. I know that the only way I can bless others is to be walking in Your blessing first.

I am a child of God and have been given the rights by spiritual birth to claim my inheritance. Because the Father loves me, I will not be denied!

Chapter Eleven

YOU ARE ALWAYS ON HIS MIND

"The LORD hath been mindful of us: he will bless us; he will bless the house of Israel; he will bless the house of Aaron. He will bless them that fear the LORD, both small and great. The LORD shall increase you more and more, you and your children."
Psalms 115:12-14 KJV

"But one in a certain place testified, saying, what is man, that thou art mindful of him? or the son of man, that thou visitest him?" Hebrews 2:6 KJV

Every day, no matter how far we have drifted from Daddy God, we are always on **His mind**. Daddy will always be mindful of us. He will always be mindful of our needs, our hurts, and our cries. God is our Father. He will always do what the father did in the story of the prodigal son. He will be waiting for our return.

"For we have not an high priest which cannot be touched with the feeling of our infirmities; but was in all points tempted like as we are, yet without sin." Hebrews 4:15 KJV

GOD FEELS OUR PAIN

Daddy God can be touched by the feelings of our infirmities. It does not matter what you are doing right now. It does not matter if you are addicted to drugs or any other type of substance abuse. It does not matter if you are divorced, or getting a divorce. The truth is that everyone in this world has experienced a train wreck in life at one time or another. What does matter is that you realize that no matter how far you have fallen, if there is still breath in your body, **there is hope to come to God**. You need to know you are on God's mind every day! God is thinking of you right now.

If you are one of the many people who have fallen and walked away from Daddy God, come home. Come to your Daddy; He is waiting on you!

You are probably not angry with God; you are probably angry at religion. The truth is God has never done anything to hurt you. God has never let you down. He has never left you nor has God forsaken you. Call to your Daddy. Tell Him you are hurting and alone. Daddy is calling for us every day. Make this the day of your return!

You will never fall too far that you would walk away from His love and mercy. The Word says, *"His mercy is new every morning."* That means today is a new day! Make it the day you come home and give everything you are facing over to daddy God.

God Loves You So Much!

When He was on the cross, you were on His mind. The only reason that Jesus stayed on that cross was that He could not get you out of His mind! There is so much love in God. Do not let religion and religious people destroy what Daddy God worked so hard to fix.

Ease the mind of God and come to Him with all your worries and cares. I promise, you will never ever regret your decision.

There is a song that I believe sums it up:

"Are you disappointed, wandering here and there, dragging chains of doubt and loaded down with cares?

Do unholy feelings struggle in your breast? Bring your cares to Jesus, He will give you rest.

Come unto me, I will give you rest. Take my yoke upon you, hear and be blessed; for I am meek and lowly, come and trust my might; come, my yoke is easy and my burden's light. "ˣˣᵛ

There is no doubt that your Heavenly Father loves you and longs to see you coming home.

Child, Come Home To Daddy! He Misses You.

Conclusion

I cannot tell you what it means to me to be able to share this message with you. I hope that it was an informative and encouraging word.

My prayer for this message is to set the captives free from the curse of illegitimacy and to set up in the mind of believers that we have the right to be blessed.

I am in no way trying to portray that I have the answers to all life's problems. I am a man who has been called by God to be a deliverer to the hurting, confused and dying.

Daddy God was birthed out of such circumstances. I have never preached this message besides the time I preached it at North Side Assembly of God. I have kept this in the safe of God until such a time as this.

People spend their whole life looking for that parent that hurt them. They search for a moment they lost in their past, chasing this memory because they lacked that nurturing love of a father. They will spend thousands of dollars sitting on a counselor's couch hoping that he or she will unlock why they feel so unfulfilled and lonely. The truth is that you cannot go back and fix what has been broken, but you can decide to start accepting who the real Father is today. He is Daddy God!

I believe that it is time for the body of Christ to understand their birthright and claim the blessings from their Daddy.

Walk in the Favor of God

Dr. Jerry Grillo

SPECİAL THAṇKS

To Dr. Mike Murdock for putting in me the inspiration to even take up the challenge of writing. Dr. Murdock, I am honored that you are my friend. Thanks for your expertise in wisdom. You are truly a man of Wisdom. My whole family loves you.

To my wife, Maryann, and my wonderful children, Jerry and Jordan, for putting up with all of my craziness. I love you dearly!

The last is the most precious to me. To my Lord and Savior Jesus, who through giving His life has allowed me the access to understand favor and the fatherhood of Daddy God. I love You with all that is in me!

May I Invite You To Make Jesus Christ The Lord Of Your Life?

The Bible says, *"That if you will confess with your mouth the Lord Jesus, and will believe in your heart that God has raised Him from the dead, you will be saved. For with the heart man believes unto righteousness; and with the mouth confession is made unto salvation."* Romans 10:9-10

Pray this prayer with me today:

"Dear Jesus, I believe that you died for me and rose again on the third day. I confess to you that I am a sinner. I need your love and forgiveness. Come into my life, forgive my sins and give me eternal life. I confess you now as my Lord. Thank you for my salvation! I walk in your peace and joy from this day forward. Daddy I am coming home! Amen!"

Signed_____

Date _____

☐ Yes, Dr. Grillo! I made a decision to accept Christ as my personal Savior today. Please send me my free gift, to help me with my journey.

Name_____

Address_____

City_____State _____ Zip _____

Phone_____ Email_____

FOGZONE MINISTRIES
P.O. Box 3707, Hickory N.C. 28603
(828) 325- 4773 Fax:(828) 325-4877
drjerrygrillo.com - drjerrygrillo@fogzone.net

[Return this page today to an usher or mail it in.]

WHAT OTHERS ARE SAYING

Dr. Jerry Grillo lives what he teaches. It has been my privilege to be his personal friend for a number of years. He is a living example of a victorious leader. His church is a victorious church. If you can't succeed under this man of God, you can't succeed anywhere. His revelation is life's fresh air in a stagnant world. He is one of the happiest and most exciting leaders I have known through my thirty-eight years of world evangelism. It is my privilege to recommend any book he has written.

Dr. Mike Murdock
The Wisdom Center
Dallas, TX

Dr. Jerry Grillo is truly a gift from God to my life. I love his passion, his purity and his painstaking commitment to purpose. It is very obvious that he loves the God he preaches to us about. Should you ever have the privilege of speaking into this life, you would know without a doubt he's one of God's favorites. Bishop Grillo, what a wonderful refreshing, what a wonderful friend!

Sheryl Brady
Sheryl Brady Ministries

Bishop Grillo is fast becoming a leading voice of authority… Having him minister at our Emotional Healing Conference became a valuable training session to our leadership and a needed breakthrough to many of our members. To say that Bishop Grillo is qualified to pen these pages would be an understatement. You hold in your hand a key to unlocking the life that God desires for you. I dare you to turn these pages with even the least little bit of expectation and watch as God begins to show out in your life!

Bishop Jeff Poole
New Hope International
Warner Robins, GA

Dr. Grillo will give you the principles to help you live a remarkable life. His keys to abundant living and success are applicable to anyone desiring to walk away from mediocrity and live life without restraints. Dr. Grillo has a profound and effective way of unfolding the scriptures so you can see God's divine plan for you to live in increase.

Kevin Mullens
Author, Mentor, Team builder, "7-figure per year earner" in
the Direct Selling Industry

If you have been looking for a shining light to cut through the fog of doubt and shine forth the F.O.G. (Favor of God), you have found it. These series of manuscripts are some of the most powerful teachings on favor that are in the Christian world today. Dr. Jerry Grillo, I believe, is one of the premier voices to this generation... Get ready; the chains of doubt, poverty and lack are about to be broken off your life.

Pastor Clint Brown
Faith World Center
Orlando, FL.

[i] James C. Dobson and Gary Lee Bauer, Children at Risk: The Battle for the Hearts and Minds of Our Kids {Nashville, TN: Word Publishing, 1990}, 205.

[ii] Ibid.

[iii] Ibid., 206.

[iv] Ibid.,9.

[v] Ibid.

[vi] Ibid.

[vii]http://bigstory.ap.org/article/172677070b1e40d7813cec2b8889b1 2f/teens-spend-average-9-hours-day-media

[viii] http://all4ed.org/reports-factsheets/the-high-cost-of-high-school-dropouts-what-the-nation-pays-for-inadequate-high-schools/

[ix] http://www.childrensdefense.org/library/moments-in-america.html?referrer=https://www.google.com/

[x] http://www.childrensdefense.org/library/state-of-americas-children/documents/2014-SOAC_child-welfare.pdf

[xi] http://www.childrensdefense.org/library/state-of-americas-children/documents/2014-SOAC_child-welfare.pdf

[xii] http://www.childrensdefense.org/library/state-of-americas-children/documents/2014-SOAC_child-welfare.pdf

[xiii] Additional information available at www.childrensdefense.org/everyday.htm.

[xiv] Thom S. Ranier, The Bridger Generation (Nashville, TN: Broadman & Holman Publishers, 1997), 76.

[xv] http://www.enlivenpublishing.com/blog/2012/09/17/4-symptoms-of-the-orphan-spirit-in-church-life/

[xvi] http://www.charismamag.com/spirit/spiritual-growth/17490-the-difference-between-the-orphan-spirit-and-a-spirit-of-sonship

[xvii] https://cbgrace.wordpress.com/2010/02/24/how-to-pray-for-an-orphan-spirit/

[xviii] https://thefatherlessgeneration.wordpress.com/statistics/

[xix] "American Agenda," World News Tonight with Peter Jennings, December 13, 1994.

[xx] "Daddy's Girl Matures Later," by Candis McLean, Report: Canada's Independent News Magazine, April 16, 2001, http://report.ca/.

[xxi] Biblesoft's New Exhaustive Strong's Numbers and Concordance with Expanded Greek-Hebrew Dictionary, copyright © 1994 Biblesoft and International Bible Translators, Inc., s.v. "lambano." All rights reserved,
[xxii] Ibid., "huiothesia."
[xxiii] http://psychcentral.com/blog/archives/2012/10/12/why-is-it-so-hard-for-men-to-cry/
[xxiv] Biblesoft's New Exhaustive Strong's Numbers and Concordance with Expanded Greek-Hebrew Dictionary, copyright © 1994 Biblesoft and International Bible Translators, Inc., s.v. "kleronomos." All rights reserved,
[xxv] "Come Unto Me," Charles P. Jones, public domain.

RELEASING THE F.O.G. FAVOR OF GOD

Dr. Jerry A. Grillo, Jr.
Author, Pastor, and Motivational Speaker

Favor Conferences - Dr. Grillo is able to minister to many during seminars and conferences throughout America and around the world. Dr. Grillo's heart is to help encourage and strengthen Senior Pastors and leaders.

Books - Dr. Grillo has written over twenty -nine books including best sellers, "Saved But Damaged," "Pray for Rain." and many others.

Internet and Television - Dr. Grillo is anointed to impart the wisdom of God on Favor, Overflow and Emotional Healing. Online streaming and television has made it possible for Dr. Grillo to carry this message around the world into homes and lives that he would otherwise not be able to reach.

FINISHED WRITING?
YOUR PUBLISHING JOURNEY IS JUST BEGINNING

Let Us Publish Your Book

FOGzone Publishing is a helpful resource for first-time authors as well as experienced authors to offer services to best help with their book. Our goal is to make your vision a reality.

Being a published author is, ultimately, all about reaching out to your readers and knowing that you're able to share your story with them. But in order to make that successful crossover from writer to published author, you need to choose the publisher that best suits your publishing goals.

It is important to publish your book with an expert publisher that will work with you from start to finish. A reputable publisher should also have the necessary experience and expertise not only in book publishing, but also in book marketing, so your book can reach the widest audience possible.

Get Started today! Contact us @ fzm@fogzone.net or 828-325-4773

WWW.DRJERRYGRILLO.COM

FOGZONE
MEDIA & DESIGNS
FOGZONE PUBLISHING
WWW.FOGZONEDESIGNS.COM

STAY**CONNECTED,**
BE**BLESSED.**

From thoughtful articles to powerful newsletters, videos and more, www.fogzone.net is full of inspirations that will give you encouragement and confidence in your daily life.

AVAILABLE ON WWW.FOGZONE.NET
to Join the FAVORNATION and receive a weekly update text the word "FAVORNATION" to 22828

LAUNCH
PASTORS AND LEADERSHIPS

Weekly Conference Calls from Dr. Grillo will help you grow in your relationship with the Lord and equip you to be everything God intends you to be.

Wednesday @ 12:00pm EST

Call: (712) 432-0075   Playback: (712) 432-1085
access CODE 138750#   access CODE 138750#

Dr. Jerry Grillo
STREAMING

Miss your local church service? Watch Dr. Grillo online, and see him LIVE.
Sundays @ 10:30am EST & Wednesday @ 7:00pm EST

Dr. Jerry Grillo
VIDEO ARCHIVE

The Video Archive is a great way to watch Dr. Grillo where you want and when you want. Go to www.drjerrygrillo.com and click on "Encore."

CONNECT WITH US

Join the FAVORNATION on your favorite social network.

PUT DR. GRILLO IN YOUR POCKET

Get the inspiration and encouragement from Dr. Jerry Grillo on your iPhone, iPad or Android device! Our website will stream on each platform.

Thanks for helping us make a difference in the lives of millions around the world.

WWW.FOGZONE.NET

WWW.DRJERRYGRILLO.COM

FOLLOW ME ON

📱 @BishopGrillo

📍 @BishopGrillo

f @BishopGrillo

▶ @Godstrongtv

Made in the USA
Lexington, KY
03 February 2018